Living According To The Circumstances

A Memoir

Noel Fernández Collot

Conversion to English: Dairy Hernandez, David Hirsch & D. H. Clark

English edition editing: Craig Henry

About this edition:

© Noel Fernández Collot, 2024.

Cover photo of Noel taken in 1999 by Michael Dunlap of the Monroe, Louisiana *News-Star*

Table of Contents

Foreword To The English Edition 1
Foreword 5
Living According To The Circumstances 17
The Family 19
The Intermediates 38
Teaching Vocation 50
Forced To Be An Accountant 64
Ideal Help 74
Military Production Assistance Units (UMAP) 92
The National Association Of The Blind 113
Ecumenism 122
Methodism 135
The Baptist Student Worker Coordination Of Cuba 145
Call To The Pastorate 166
The Emmanuel Baptist Church 175
Missionary Work 188
The Fraternity Of Baptists Churches Of Cuba (FIBAC) 209
The Pastoral Care Of People With Disabilities 217
Joni And Friends - JAF 243
Beyond The Seas 251
The Ecumenical Network In Defense Of The People With Disabilities (EDAN) 280
Native Peoples In Latin America 292
My Four Pastors 298
Afterword To The English Edition 317
About The Author 323

Foreword To The English Edition

It has been my privilege to introduce this book at several of the presentations of the book in Cuba. Hopefully, the following words from those introductions will be an adequate foreword to this English edition.

With fear and trembling, I thank Noel for the invitation to present his autobiographical book, although I don't think that after my presentation, he will continue to think that it was a good idea!

I believe that when it comes to books, there are two important things to keep in mind: #1, the author, and #2, the content of the book.

Regarding the first, I can tell you that we have had the historical privilege of having known an exceptional human being, an exceptionality that jumps out in every word of this book titled *Living According to the Circumstances*. This is because precisely the circumstances that Noel has had to overcome in his life, have not been easy: the misunderstandings, the exclusions, the rejections of individuals and social structures that this man has suffered. These would have led any normal human being to suicide or a "catastrophic implosion" like that of the submarine Titan, but neither these nor the loss of his sight have made any dent in this man. Well, that is except for some outbursts and sharpness that characterize him. Although my mother said that these had nothing to do with any of these situations, they were part of his character, which was the same from a very young age when she first met him, and yet, his circumstances had not gotten bad.

But well, as his detractors might say, "Through tantrums and fights," Noel has known how to turn circumstances, often adverse, into steps by which he has known how to climb, with dignity and sacrifice, towards a top place in the history of the church in our country. He has left behind a trail of great works in favor of social justice, the improvement of relations between the church and the State, and inclusion and dignified treatment for people with disabilities, all of which are masterfully narrated in the pages of this book.

As a Christian, I understand that The Gospel, that is, the Good News of God in Christ, is precisely the certainty that the world can change, and that human beings can change. And not just that they can change but they can also make that change real in the world, in the lives of human beings. That change has become real in the author of this book, who has known how, despite adversity, to break through and achieve victories that give birth to love, peace, and justice. These are the pillars of that better world, which the Bible includes in the Kingdom of God. They are also Good News. They are the living Gospel.

Regarding the book, I can tell you that it has a little of everything. It may be outrageous for some who do not share his opinion on some issues discussed here: "of that patriotic, transformative, renewing and radical fervor, nothing remains, and of the social impact, political, theological, ecclesiological, there's not much left." It has intrigues: "Samuel and Melvin established a deep relationship of affection," adult language: "How do you think I'm going to feel in this shit," and the occasional fib: "...the church of which I am now a part, without interfering in any of its administrative and organizational aspects".

But if you are more given to those romance stories and a little something more "spicy" in the book, you can find ideal help--everything that contributes to making reading it very interesting and enjoyable.

On the other hand, and more seriously, it is one of the few books published in our country that contains experiential details and addresses the issue of some Cuban social stages that many circles of power and decision-makers would like to be forgotten, such as the Military Production Support Units, UMAP, which Noel suffered firsthand.

This volume in question not only sheds light on the life of its author but also, through it, we can see the historical pilgrimage of the church in Cuba and the evolution of the dynamic of the relationship between it and the state.

Living According to the Circumstances

Regarding this last aspect, being here today, in this institution [the House of Cultural Diversity], presenting this book, written by a Baptist pastor, constitutes a fact of hope and victory for those of us who, because of this, still continue to fight and remain dissatisfied with what has been achieved so far by the generation of the author of this book.

Reading this book can be like going on a roller coaster in an amusement park. Sometimes, you may laugh out loud, but other times, you could cry as you become sensitive to some of the "circumstances" experienced by Noel. In short, there is everything that an excellent book should contain. It is a book that we recommend and will promote, always with the aim that those who do so can come to understand that life and the future belong to those who, like Noel, despite the circumstances, fight and prevail to make things happen. They do not stop to become depressed and languish in the self-pity of what happens to them.

Thank you, Noel, for bequeathing your edifying and controversial experiences in this book but also in the achievements of your struggle, which have been, and continue to be, your life.

Eduardo González Hernández

Ciego de Avila, Cuba

August 1, 2024

Foreword

Throughout my pastoral life and my work in the ecumenical movement, I have met many brothers and sisters with disabilities, but my faith and trust in God have been strengthened even more by the life, testimony, and friendship of an exceptional person, namely, the brother, pastor, and graduate in accounting, Noel Osvaldo Fernández Collot.

The pages of this book attest to this, which is a mandatory reference to learn more first-hand about the Christian witness in a socialist society, about the work of the churches, and, more particularly, about the issue of people with disabilities, not only in Cuba but also in Latin America and worldwide.

In this sense, the volume is of great formative value, particularly for the new generations of Christians who did not live the experiences of those first three decades of the Revolution in which a severe State atheism was imposed on us, in contrast to the openness which occurred in the 1990s, when a secular state was adopted, which led to a fuller participation of churches in our society.

The purpose of this work is defined by the author when he comments in the first chapter, "I learned to face changes, to accept them as God's challenges for my life and to direct myself along new paths, seeking and creating the best alternatives, not merely to survive, but to serve with accumulated experiences.

That's what I'm trying to share in this book." So, we are faced with the text of a person who, as a result of his Christian faith, has enjoyed a life of hope and optimism, even in the midst of great adversity, some of which are explained in this book.

I have often reflected on the difference between having the sense of sight, on the one hand, and having vision, on the other. The latter refers to the ability to conceive the future reality as long as it is considered the type of action carried out with imagination, wisdom, and confidence.

Vision motivates a utopian gaze that makes us move forward;[1] it is the driving force and one of the essential foundations of our existence. According to Judeo-Christian tradition, this is crucial, "For where there is no vision, the people perish" (Pr 29:18a). How many people do we know who, enjoying the sense of sight, lose the meaning of life because they lack this vision? I have shared with Noel that even when he lost his sense of sight, his vision prevails firmly, anchored in the faith *of* Christ (not just faith *in* Christ), as he himself frequently mentions, focused on the reign of God, which according to the

---

[1] As the Uruguayan writer Eduardo Galeano said, "Utopia is on the horizon. I take two steps closer, it takes two steps away. I walk ten steps and the horizon moves ten steps further. No matter how much I walk, I will never reach it. So, for what does the utopia works? For that: it serves to make us move forward." (http://www.goodreads.com/quotes /33846-utopia-lies-at-the-horizon-when-i-draw-nearer-by).

Apostle Paul, it is a matter of "...justice, peace and joy in the Holy Spirit" (Rom 14:17).

Noel begins his book by arguing about the importance of the family and the influence it had on his formation and genetic transmission, as he informs us that "we have all lost our sense of sight as a result of a degenerative disease known as retinitis pigmentosa." Knowing this background helps us understand him better as a person and understand more clearly the ideas of this volume, especially with regard to the treatment of the issue of people with disabilities. We observe how the author develops a series of tasks that attest to his diverse and multifaceted vocations, all at the service of a living gospel present in society. After sharing in detail about his studies, it is interesting to read about his different work experiences, starting with teaching work and then as an accountant "by force," as he himself explains to us.

In all fairness and justice, he dedicates an entire chapter and countless references to his life partner, Ormara Nolla Cao, whom he calls a "help mate" (in allusion to Genesis 2:18), who has provided for Noel for almost sixty years (since his marriage in 1965) adequate and fundamental support for the different ministries and tasks that he has carried out, in my opinion, assigned by God. Undoubtedly, she was a vital support when Noel lost his sense of sight, but even before, as a companion on the journey and in service, all this without neglecting her own responsibilities in the provincial library of Camagüey, in the church, in the Council of Churches of Cuba and in the World Day of Prayer program, in which she played very prominent roles, among other responsibilities. It is worth noting here, in a similar way, the "help mate" that, I am sure, Noel has been for Ormara: they are an exemplary couple who complement each other.

Another aspect that stands out is Noel's ecumenical vocation and commitment. Although he received a denominational Christian education, his vision on the matter expanded thanks to his relationship with brothers and sisters of various confessions. He states that he came to understand "the value of unity in the midst of diversity, and the need for a testimony in which the acceptance of the point of view and interpretation of the other will be valued instead of denigrated." As you will see, this logic of respect and acceptance of the other person even goes beyond the interdenominational relations of Christian churches to encompass a broader ecumenism that embraces even secular or non-governmental institutions.

In this sense, Noel manifests himself as a pioneer, as founder or co-founder of several relevant organizations, by becoming co-initiator of the National Association of the Blind (ANCI) in the province of Ciego de Ávila, the Baptist Student Workers Coordination of Cuba (COEBAC), the Ecumenical

Network for the Defense of Persons with Disabilities (EDAN) and the World Council of Churches, among others.

One trait of Noel's personality that is emphasized in the book is his perseverance and hope. When describing to us the harshness of his experiences in the UMAP (Military Production Assistance Units), his first assessment is one of persistence and optimism: instead of complaining, he thanks God for the experience and for the learning. It reminded me of my own experience in the Youth Army of Labor, a descendant of the UMAP, in which, although with non-comparable living conditions - they improved in later editions - I was recruited for the same reason as Noel.

Of all the vocations mentioned by the author, perhaps the one to which he dedicates the most time and space is that of pastor. In this regard, he highlights that after many years, I understood that being a pastor is not only and exclusively being in charge of the spiritual guidance of a church, but rather it is guiding, especially by example, people who are in the area of influence of the pastor. It is worth saying that Noel not only understood this definition of a pastor, but he practiced it, especially among the most marginalized people. The fact of having suffered separation from the membership of the First Baptist Church of Ciego de Ávila in 1978 and other responsibilities in the Baptist Convention of Eastern Cuba led him to pastor others who had suffered the same fate. The fact of having suffered expulsion from both levels of the Baptist Church made Pastor Noel even more aware of the defense of vulnerable and marginalized people, of those who had suffered similar experiences, as Jesus of Nazareth himself did, and also strengthened in him greater ecumenical commitment.

Significant, in this sense, is the founding of the Emmanuel Baptist Church on November 13, 1994, and a year later, his ordination and commission in this congregation as its pastor, with a marked style of "worker priest," a notion that he mentions three times. I stop here to delve into the meaning of the church's name: Emmanuel is "God with us." This is eloquently summed up by Noel when he writes that the congregation "... more than fulfilled its purpose and opened a new intentionality of service and a new expression of faith, not known before in the city." And, thanks to diaconal work, we feel closer to God, and we approach God in a more tangible way through other people, especially the most vulnerable.

In this regard, the book relates a whole list of diaconal works developed by the Emmanuel Church, namely, attention to a group of Alcoholics Anonymous (the first in the province of Ciego de Ávila) and, almost in parallel, a program of pastoral care that met for the elderly every Thursday, which was called The Golden Age. Every year since 1997, they make a basket that is delivered on December 25th to the first infant who needs it the most and is born that day. Other community outreach efforts have been the Good Samaritan Pantry and the sewing workshop, as well as a library specialized in subjects related to religion, at the service of secular researchers, religious leaders of the city, and the large family of Emmanuel Church.

How to achieve all this? An essential component in the work of the Church is a spirituality of commitment. An example of this was the need to acquire a new property. Noel writes in this regard that "the place became too small for us, and we began to dream first, to work later and to always pray... On September 15, 1996, we dedicated to the Lord the building that today is our house of prayer... God answered our prayers."

Another important aspect of the work of this congregation has been its missionary outreach. The author says, "There were eighteen places where we established missionary work in the province of Ciego de Ávila between 1992 and 2001. Six churches emerged from that work: La Vid Verdadera in Corojo, Getsemaní in Colorado, Koinonia in Pesquería, Gabaón in La Ilusión, Betania in Chambas, and Canaán in Bolivia. They all managed to acquire their own place for their activities, and in less than ten years, they also had a permanent worker in pastoral work."

The pastor and the parishioners were not content with the work of his congregation, limited to the city of Ciego de Ávila, but inspired by Acts 1:8 and other missionary biblical texts, they have been motivated by the Holy Spirit, who provides them with the power to be witnesses of Jesus Christ not only in the place where the "mother" temple is located but in other locations that require the message of his gospel.

Noel concluded his pastorate in May 2009, when the Church installed Eduardo González Hernández as pastor upon his request to cease active service.

Starting in 1989, when Noel almost completely lost his sense of sight, he received a new ministry from God. He says that he thought about the need to encourage an adequate policy of pastoral care and inclusion of people with disabilities in Cuban Churches. In 1992, a department called Coordination for the Disabled was created in the Council of Churches, of which Noel was appointed director.

Among the emphases of this department, one of the most appreciated is the biblical-theological formation of people with disabilities, which has been hard work carried out with the theology seminaries. As a consequence, the topic has been a priority for our Evangelical Theology Seminary (SET for its acronym in Spanish). There have been many achievements in this regard, among which is the revision of the curriculum to more intentionally incorporate this topic, as well as other special activities such as training seminars for leaders with disabilities and the training of guides-interpreters for deaf/blind people from the Cuban Churches, as well as national and international events and forums. We highlight the joint project SET, the

Living According to the Circumstances

Biblical Commission of the Council of Churches of Cuba, and the United Bible Societies of a Bible translation work. It is important to add that the SET has as part of its annual programming a day dedicated to the topic of disability with the title Day of the Gifts of People with Disabilities. The SET highly values and recognizes the work of our brother Noel and his team, which has very positively influenced our work of forming new generations of theologians, male and female pastors, who facilitate the work of raising awareness and training in more inclusive churches, that more comprehensively incorporate the gifts of all our brothers and sisters with disabilities.

On February 12, 2019, the Board of Directors of the Council of Churches of Cuba received, through the national team of the Pastoral Care of People with Disabilities, the request for the release of the general coordinator of the program and the recommendation to appoint Master of Sciences Rolando Verdecia Ávila to that position. There were almost twenty-nine years of beautiful work in which this program achieved significant impacts.

As I was a member of the Board of Directors, I vividly remember our discussions when people had to cease their work in the different departments and commissions of the Council of Churches of Cuba (CIC for its acronym in Spanish) for a regular period of time. We always found arguments for, in an exceptional way, our brother Noel to continue coordinating this

Pastoral until our brother Rolando Verdecia, the current coordinator of it arrived.

Brother Noel's networking work has also been very important, not only with the Churches – even non-members of the CIC – but with other secular or non-governmental institutions such as, for example, the Cuban Association of People with Physical-Motor Limitations (ACLIFIM), with which he collaborated in the distribution of wheelchairs to more than seven thousand people, each of whom received a Bible. This project was carried out with the support of the Joni and Friends (JAF) project from the United States. Noel and his team served as intermediaries between both organizations, all in favor of these people in need, most of whom have expressed their gratitude and interest in the gospel of Jesus Christ.

I highlight another no less important profile of Noel's service, this time as ambassador of the Cuban ecumenical movement in the world. Just to cite one example, he had the opportunity to serve global ecumenism through his participation in three areas of the World Council of Churches.

The first, very prominent, was the Ecumenical Network in Defense of Persons with Disabilities (EDAN), of which he was coordinator for Latin America for eighteen years and, for ten years, a member of its international coordination group. He was also a member of the Justice, Peace, and Integrity of Creation (JPC) unit and the Commission of International Affairs (CCIA), an important sphere of the world's largest ecumenical movement.

In his work with EDAN on our continent, again, his emphasis on biblical-theological training was present, which is why he visited many theological seminaries in the region. Here and in other areas, the experiences with the CIC's Ministry of People with Disabilities were of immense help to him. Thus, a specific objective that guided the work of the Network in Latin America was to promote the curricular inclusion of disability in theological institutions. To this end, promotional activities and visits were carried out to several of them.

It is worth highlighting the author's efforts in favor of the "doubly marginalized." In the traditional Latin American context, women occupy a very secondary place in society and even in the Churches, but if these women are also indigenous or Afro-descendant, marginalization is greater. And, of course, if living with a disability is added to these two elements, the effect is immense. Faced with this situation, the Network has carried out various tasks to creatively deal with this situation, recognizing the dignity and condition of each human being in the image of God. Noel's commitment and solidarity in favor of marginalized people is also confirmed by his relationship with the indigenous peoples in Latin America, to whom he dedicates a chapter of the book that ends with this phrase: "Latin American Christians have a great debt to our original ancestors. I believe that it is essential to think about ways, means, and procedures through which we learn from their cultures, traditions, and beliefs."

Noel and his EDAN team organized a series of regional consultations, the last of which was held in Santiago de Chile in October 2012. I was very privileged to be invited by him while serving the World Council of Churches as coordinator of relations with churches and related institutions in Latin America and the Caribbean. I was in charge of the sermon at the closing service, which I titled "Inclusive communities to carry out God's commission." I concluded with a prayer in which I cited, in relation to EDAN, the declaration "The Church of All," adopted in 2003 by the Central Committee of the World Council of Churches. Therefore, I end this foreword by repeating this prayer in order to entrust to God this work of his servant Noel.

Let us pray: "Let us, O God, who are created in your image, reflect your compassion, creativity, and imagination as we work to reorganize our society, our buildings, our programs, and our liturgy so that everyone can participate. In you, we are no longer alone but united in one body. Trusting in your wisdom and your grace, we pray gratefully in the name of Jesus, Amen."

Carlos Emilio Ham Stanard

Matanzas, Cuba

December 25, 2021

Living According To The Circumstances

It is uncomfortable for me to hear people who do not personally experience any kind of disability say that it entails suffering. The reality is that every person, with or without disabilities, can suffer. People with a sensory, physical, or cognitive disability can be long-suffering or enterprising, happy, and jovial. It all depends on our circumstances and the understanding we have of life. The "abundant life" that Jesus Christ offers (John 10:10) is not limited to the standards of beauty and quality imposed by our culture. Always living with joy, hope, and gratitude to God for life is an attitude acquired, instilled, and assimilated.

Those who live with discontent, sadness, and suffering, even without being considered disabled, carry with them the worst of disabilities. We must learn to "laugh with those who laugh" without forgetting to "cry with those who cry," to approach people with disabilities from the perspective of equal opportunities and to understand that we are in the presence of human beings as different as any other.

Being blind, deaf, or a person with any other disability is but one of the many ways of life that exist in the world created by God. No two human beings are alike. Appreciating differences and striving to understand them brings us closer to understanding that we all must learn to live with or without disabilities. In this sense, Saint Paul's experience is paradigmatic: imprisoned in a maximum-security prison, tied with chains to a Roman guard, sentenced to death, close to the third age and with low vision, he was able to write to the church of Philippi: "crown and joy of his salvation" and "...I know how to live whatever the circumstances...".

The generation of which I am part has experienced ever-changing situations. For me, the "road to Damascus" was not, as for Saint Paul, the knowledge of the saving grace of Jesus Christ. Political, social, economic, religious, and vocational changes came to me at different times and taught me to live in abundance and in scarcity, to live whatever the circumstances. I learned to face changes, to accept them as God's challenges for my life, and to take new paths, seeking and creating the best alternatives, not merely to survive but to serve with accumulated experiences. That is what I try to share in this text.

Already entering the so-called third age, when I look back, I have nothing left but the satisfaction of having fulfilled my duty, gratitude to the Lord for the abilities and strength to live in different circumstances, and the certainty that everything is possible through Christ who gives us the power.

Ciego de Avila, Cuba

September 2019

The Family

I was born on February 28, 1942, into two very different families. My father, Eduardo Eugenio Fernández Borrero, was the son of Eduardo and María, first cousins. Two of my grandfather's brothers also married two first cousins. In short, my great-grandparents had three Fernández sons married to three Borrero daughters.

This gave rise to a defect that meant that in the family – very large, by the way – there were a large number of people with visual disabilities. We all have lost our sense of sight as a result of a degenerative disease known as retinitis pigmentosa. The disease is incurable but usually manifests itself in adulthood. In our country, the ophthalmologist Dr. Orfilio Peláez Molina dedicated all his efforts to researching this ailment. In 1987, Dr. Peláez began performing a surgical treatment that he believed could stop the progression of blindness in those suffering from retinitis. What was achieved by this eminent man of science had an international scope.

One Sunday in the summer of 1996, at the end of the liturgical celebration at the Northminster Church in Monroe, Louisiana, with which our church has a pact of brotherhood, and where I was visiting accompanied by my wife, a lady was waiting for me at the church door to thank me for the treatment she received in Cuba for her visual condition, which had managed to stop the progression of her disease.

I was one of Dr. Peláez's first patients at the Salvador Allende hospital in Havana. I was hospitalized for a week to receive the treatment. Unfortunately, I did not have a positive result because an acute glaucous attack in the left eye first and a week later in the right eye led to complete blindness.

During my stays in that hospital and later in the clinic for the care of people with retinitis pigmentosa, a Public Health institution created in each provincial capital at the initiative of Dr. Peláez, I had many relationships with people who, like me, were treated there. It was a magnificent opportunity to share the feeling of hope that we learn from our walk through life holding the hand of the Lord.

But let's go back to my paternal family. Dad was the eldest of five male brothers – Luis, Carlos, Joaquín, and Rubén – and three female sisters: María Rosa, Alicia, and Luz Marina. Of them, Carlos, Joaquín, Rubén, María Rosa, and Luz Marina lost their sight as a result of retinitis pigmentosa.

My father, an entrepreneur, cultured and educated, traveled at the age of eighteen with one of his cousins, Mario Herrera Fernández, to the United States. They settled in New York, where they deepened their knowledge of English and learned about the culture and customs of that country. My father talked about his sadness at the prevailing discrimination, of which he was also the object, in the 1920s and part of the 1930s when he worked and lived there. He instilled in us, perhaps unintentionally, a feeling of rejection of the American way of life.

Upon their return from the United States, both cousins settled in Havana and my father contracted his first marriage, which he almost never spoke about. His failed marriage took him to Camagüey, his native land, where he met my mother one Sunday night in Agramonte Park.

At that time, young men and women went to hear the concerts played by the Municipal Concert Band at seven pm. My mother, accompanied by other girls from the church, left the park a little before eight to walk a hundred meters that separate it from the First Baptist Church and arrive on time for Sunday worship. My father followed the group of young girls... and the crush occurred.

Mom's relationship with a divorced man eleven years older than her was not well regarded in the family, but my father's education and the couple's persistence broke down the wall of incomprehension. They contracted a civil marriage in Camagüey in 1935, but they held the religious ceremony at the First Baptist Church of Ciego de Ávila, where I would also celebrate my nuptials. They had decided to do it there because Reverend Guillermo Rodríguez, who had been a pastor for several years in Camagüey and at that time was working in Ciego de Ávila, was their spiritual guide.

My father, who worked almost his entire working life in the Camagüey railway company with North American capital, achieved important positions thanks to his intelligence and extensive command of English. His premature retirement in 1952 due to loss of sight put us at a financial disadvantage. We were used to living on my father's magnificent salary plus what my mother earned as an employee of the Provincial Superintendency of Schools.

Dad's forced retirement was followed by my mother's dismissal. One year after Fulgencio Batista's coup d'état, on March 10, 1952, all public employees were required to join a provincial act in support of the de facto regime. My mother refused to participate and made statements against the dictatorship. In less than twenty-four hours, she was fired. Our economic situation, already precarious, worsened even more when, due to embezzlement in the Railway Retirement Fund, my father did not receive his pension during the last four months of 1958.

Dad took pleasure in caring for his family, visiting them, encouraging them, and collaborating as much as possible with those who lived in more disadvantaged situations than us. I remember that when he was already blind, he went out every day, from Monday to Friday, to visit a different relative. Even today, I don't know how Dad, being completely blind, had acquired such a capacity for orientation and mobility without passing any school. He especially visited his blind brothers and sisters and his many cousins who also lived in total darkness. His visits, more than family visits, were pastoral because he always brought them a message of encouragement and hope. Everyone enjoyed his optimism and positive sense of life. I have never heard him deny his situation or appear desperate. He instilled peace and serenity.

After his retirement, Dad had a visual residue that helped him orient himself. He lost it the day he accompanied on foot, from the Guernica district, in the north of the city, to the general cemetery, in the south, the body of his sister-in-law Zenaida Pérez, the wife of his younger brother, Ruben. My father commented that the sun in front of him on that long trip dazzled him in such a way that when he arrived at the cemetery, he could not see anything, and he had to ask his brother Luis, who never suffered from his eyesight, to accompany him home.

I remember that the next day, two things happened that marked me. The first was that, after lunch, Dad got up from the table to look for the refrigerator to pour himself a glass of water. My brother ran to do it for him. My father, with his usual sweetness, told him: "No, leave me alone. Today, you can help me, but I won't always have someone to help me." That same afternoon, Dad went out to the sidewalk, and with a cane that my maternal uncle, Juan Collot, had brought him as a gift early in the morning, he arrived in front of the door of the pharmacy that was on the corner. He stood there, trying to cross the street. The pharmacist who owned the establishment, Dr. Pío Delio González, left his job and came to the aid of my father, who kindly told him: "Thank you very much, Pío, but let me do it alone. I have to learn to stand up for myself." I, had left the house after Dad, fearing that something would happen to him, did not dare to intervene. I just watched and prayed.

Dad's family was made up of hard-working men and women, lovers of relationships of companionship and brotherhood and with a great sense of honesty and love for great causes. Some confessed to be Catholics. Until his death, which occurred in the United States, Rubén was a faithful Jehovah's Witness. My father was the only one who had an interpretation of life in accordance with the teachings of the evangelical and Protestant churches, learned in his youth, during his residence in the United States.

My mother's family was very different. Mom was the daughter of Juan Collot Montejo and América Pérez Guzmán. The history of the Collot family dates back to the end of the 18th century. According to stories that have come down to us by oral transmission, my great-great-grandfather, Jean Marie Collot (he had not yet incorporated D'Herbois into his surname), was imbued with the Enlightenment spirit of the 18th century and finished secondary school being an assiduous reader of Voltaire and encyclopedias, a habit in which a Parisian neighbor helped him initiate.

In that pre-revolutionary time, he joined traveling provincial theaters and became a theater director in Geneva. He joined a young woman with artistic aspirations – a comedian, they would have said at the time – from Nice. This relationship had no known offspring, which does not invalidate the probable existence of "natural" children of our ancestors welcomed by his "legitimate" wife already at the time of his meteoric political rise during the Revolution.

When the French Revolution triumphed, Jean Marie appeared in Paris and began an evolution parallel to the radicalization of the process: from monarchical parliamentarian to the presidency of the National Assembly and the request for the guillotine for Louis XVI, passing through stages of literary popularity, activism Jacobin politician, close relationship with Robespierre and very fraternal friendship with Billaud-Varenne, including a failed assassination attempt in his apartment by a counter-revolutionary terrorist, from which he escaped safely because the detonators of the murderer's two revolvers jammed.

Two significant events at that time were the advertising success of his Atheist Almanac, which won a contest to catechize peasants in the ideals of the French Revolution, and the massacre of the Lyon rebels, with heavy artillery, in the time of terror, with the sponsorship and sinister company of Fouché.

Later, together with Billaud-Varenne, he would save his head from the guillotine by being deported to Cayenne just moments before the acolytes on duty of the Terror signed his death sentence. In Cayenne, our ancestor won over the revolutionary garrison, fraternized with the sisters of the hospital during the time of fever, was considered a hero by the captain of the garrison, and even managed to get involved in a slave uprising with the sublime rhetoric of freedom, equality and brotherhood of the Declaration of the Rights of Man and Citizen.

His death certificate is so ambiguous that it seems more like a safe-conduct document for escape, and it was not signed by the fort's official doctor but by someone who happened to be replacing him that day.

This is the point where legend and reality meet.

French historiography culminates the story of this character in Cayenne, former French Guiana, but since my childhood I heard various family stories about Jean Marie. According to oral tradition, he changed his clothes and made a "smuggling" journey through the Caribbean until he founded his Cuban family. In Port-au-Prince, he married Ángela de Miranda, the illegal daughter of a Catholic priest. There, he built the house that would be the family's refuge for more than two centuries –

and which is still standing – at 53 Astilleros Street between San Miguel and Lugareño, and he baptized his four children in the parish of Santa Ana, two blocks from his house.[2]

Perhaps the most evident proof that my maternal family descends from such a complicated character is the impetuous, bold, dynamic, and intransigent character of its members, to which is added their love for politics.

My mother had three brothers: Prisciliano, Juan, and Enrique. The first and the last were representatives of the Chamber for the Authentic Revolutionary Party. My uncle Enrique had previously been a municipal councilor in the Camagüey City Council and had a flourishing political, radical, and truly revolutionary life. He was always, like Prisciliano later, on the most left wing of the Party. Unfortunately, on April 16, 1950, he died in an accident that occurred when the plane in which he was flying from the city of Morón to Camagüey took off, another legislator, Carlos Álvarez Recio, as well as Mario Fernández, candidate for mayor of Santa Cruz del Sur, and four other people, were traveling. The funeral, attended by President Carlos Prío Socarrás and to which one hundred and fifty-six floral offerings were sent, shook the entire city, and especially my family. Still today, in the Plaza de San Ramón, very close to the house where he, his two brothers, and my mother were

---

[2] Taken from a historical investigation about Jean María Collot carried out by my nephew Eduardo V. Fernández Fernández.

born, a monument stands in his memory, built by popular subscription shortly after his death.

The physical disappearance of my uncle Enrique significantly affected my grandmother and my mother, who began to suffer from frequent depression. For this reason, the specialist in nerve pathways, as psychiatrists were then called, recommended a vacation and a change of activity. We went to the United States for the second time the following year, which encouraged her a lot and allowed her to join her work again. That trip also served to accompany my brother to the *Toccoa Fall Institute*, an institution of the Presbyterian Church where he would attend high school. Two years earlier, in 1949, we had traveled to that country for the first time to be treated by Dr. Castro Viejo, a famous New York ophthalmologist of the time. He diagnosed that neither my brother nor I had any vision problems but that there was no solution for my father's advanced vision deterioration.

Prisciliano, my other representative uncle, had a very different character from Enrique: he was loquacious, friendly, and popular, but also intransigent and transformative. He was a combative legislator who strove to obtain the rights, even taken away by his own party, from the popular classes, especially the workers. He was surprised by the performance of his position by the disastrous coup of March 10, 1952, with which Fulgencio Batista was installed in power. A phone call to his house on

Lugareño Street on the corner of Rancho Boyeros Avenue in Havana, at dawn that day, from the Minister of Education of Carlos Prío's cabinet, Aureliano Sánchez Arango, informed him of what was happening in Columbia. Without thinking twice, he headed to the Presidential Palace to find out the president's opinion. Other members of political life were arriving at the Palace. Some of them, among whom was my uncle Prisciliano, voted to resist the coup and prevent Batista's inauguration. Prío, hesitant and timid, told them: "I don't want a bloodbath in Cuba, that's what you propose." The president left the Presidential Palace in my uncle Prisciliano's black Buick bound for the embassy of Mexico, where he sought political asylum.

My uncle Prisciliano fought alongside other politicians of the same tendency during the first years of the dictatorship, then he took refuge in his house in Santa Cruz del Sur, surrounded by friends and books, to live peacefully and always with optimism. There are countless anecdotes that I keep about him, full of the Creole humor that characterized him. I have memories and great lessons from him and Enrique.

My other uncle, Juan, who did not stand out in political life, was an important character in the family due to his austerity and creativity. Like Enrique, he had no children, but he made his four nephews – Juan Oscar and Isabel América, children of Prisciliano, and my brother Eduardín and I – his most precious treasures. I have no complaints about any of my three uncles.

Living According to the Circumstances

It wouldn't be fair if I didn't mention my aunts-in-law. The three of them were very different: Rosa Carmenate was also involved in politics, although after the death of my uncle Enrique when the most honest part of the country's public life rejected that option as a solution to Batista's dictatorial imprint. Luz Sánchez, Prisciliano's wife, was popular, expressive and daring. Giselda Rodríguez was my second mother: she loved us all in a very unique way, and she was someone whose advice and guidance was always taken into account in the family.

My mother was a sum of the indomitable, restless, dynamic, and bold character of the Collot family succession. I have often wondered how my parents, with such a different background and characteristics, were able to love and understand each other so much. Mom was the only one who followed the evangelical teachings of my grandmother, América, one of the first women baptized in the First Baptist Church of Camagüey at the beginning of the 20th century. Mom was baptized at the age of fourteen, and she was faithful to the teachings she received until she departed to the presence of the Lord in September 1999.

Mom worked at the Provincial Superintendence of Schools. She had tried to graduate from the Normal School of Teachers, which she did not achieve, but her job was, while she was able to do it, in the branch of education.

Living According to the Circumstances

Dad's death on April 2, 1975, and that of my only brother, Eduardín, a few hours after returning from Dad's funeral, once again exacerbated her nervous depression and her permanent sadness. I think there were many reasons: her father's infidelity to my grandmother, the hardships of a divided home, the economic hardship that forced her brothers to become cigar makers and her to place bands on the cigars in her early youth, the loss of her youngest brother, and her husband and her son almost simultaneously affected her mind and her heart.

The Christian education I received was fundamentally what my maternal grandmother, América Pérez Guzmán, transmitted to me. According to her time, she was a recalcitrant Baptist: there was no other salvation than professing the tradition, principles, and doctrines preached by her denomination. She was deeply anti-Catholic. She often said that her father, who had left Cuba at the end of the Ten Years' War and returned during the Peace of Zanon, had married, and his first daughter had been born. Since there was no Civil Registry in the country, he had to baptize her in the Catholic church of Güines. The priest prevented him from naming her America, as he wanted, so in order to baptize her, he had to choose a name from the Catholic saints. Outraged, my great-grandfather told the priest, "Well, name her María Francisca Paula de la Caridad América," and that was my good grandmother's name.

Living According to the Circumstances

My great-grandfather, as I said, was apparently forced to leave the country at the end of the Ten Years' War but returned during the period known as the Fertile Truce, in which many of the emigrants returned, mostly with the intention of continuing the patriotic fight against Iberian domination. He was arrested for conspiring against Spanish domination, but released shortly before the War of Independence, he joined the Cuban ranks.

The "guerrillas" (voluntary allies of the Spanish forces) burned his house and peasant farm, so the rest of the family had to take up residence in the city of Camagüey, not far from the farm. My great-grandfather died in combat against the Spanish army a few weeks after his uprising. Nobody wanted to tell his wife, Magdalena, who was sick at the time, the disastrous news, but someone who visited her indiscreetly mentioned it. My great-grandmother died a few days later, and my grandmother, América, the eldest of the daughters, took care of her brothers and sisters: Recardo, Oscar, César Augusto, Emma, Ofelia, Amanda, Zelmira, and Adela. Adela was adopted by an American couple during the first intervention of the United States in Cuba, she traveled with them to that northern country, and her family never heard from her again.

My only brother, five years older than me, trained under the same concepts and the same discipline, was diametrically opposed to me. After completing his studies at Upper Primary School number 5, he left the First Baptist Church of Camagüey, in which the entire family participated, to join the congregation of the Evangelical Pentecostal Church, Assemblies of God, which was in the process of building its temple in Havana Square. His justification, although it was credible, had no weight for the family members, "I want to be part of a church where the fire of the Holy Spirit is felt." A few months after he joined that congregation, my father decided that he would go to the United States to complete his high school diploma. Halfway through the course, he wrote home requesting permission to enroll in the seminary: "I want to become a pastor." Dad congratulated him for his initiative but told him that he would not see a cent if he gave up his high school studies: "When you finish your high school, I am pleased that you study at the seminary, before that, don't count on us," my father wrote to him.

At the end of the course, when he came home on vacation, my brother did not return to the church nor became more interested in religious topics. He told my aunt Giselda when she rebuked him for that decision: "I want to know the world, I want to enjoy life, I want to have a conversion experience, something worthy of repentance...".

My brother did not study the third and last year of high school in the United States. Dad wanted him to incorporate the British accent of the English language, and to do so, he enrolled him at Calabar School in Kingston, Jamaica. However, he did not complete high school at that institution because he fell ill with typhus and returned to Cuba. From then on, my brother's health was always very broken, which was accompanied by a youth full of emotional imbalances. Someone said in the family that he was the closest heir of Jean María Collot d'Herbois.

Out of fear of Batista's repression against youth and because of the involvement that Eduardín was having in the insurrectional fight against the dictatorship, my parents decided that he return to the United States. First, he went to New York, where he worked in several hotels, and later to Montreal, Canada, avoiding the US Army draft. In Canada he managed to work in one of the best hotels in Montreal, the Ritz Carlton, which allowed him economic well-being that he quickly wasted.

He returned to Cuba at the triumph of the Revolution on January 23, 1959. His return, full of optimism and hope for the Cuban future, delighted the rest of the family, who agreed with his opinions. The family was surprised by his assertion that "what is needed here is to follow the model of European communism, that is the solution to our problems." Nobody agreed, but in no more than three years, that was the option, chosen or forced, of the Cuban Revolution. Eduardín became totally involved in the political tasks of the time and became a founder of the Cuban Communist Party. I believe that he was sincere and consistent with his ideals and, in addition, very respectful of the points of view of my parents, whom he always

Living According to the Circumstances

encouraged to maintain their convictions and participate in the life of the church.

Little by little, we identified ourselves, and got closer, even when we did not agree on some criteria of the Cuban revolution. With each passing year, we looked for more coincidences and common points in our conversations. I think his affection for me was much greater than what I showed him; his personality made it possible. He was also much more expressive with my parents than I was. The final result of his existence is that he was a son, a brother, and an exemplary citizen.

My brother left only one son, Eduardo Vladimir Fernández Fernández, whom he loved very much, although an early divorce deprived him of the privilege of having him by his side. This only descendant of the family studied Philosophy at a Moscow university, graduated with high grades, and worked at the University of Camagüey as a professor of Ethics and Marxist Aesthetics, but decided to stay and reside in Costa Rica when he went to take a course in that country. My nephew has surpassed his father and even his grandfather in ability, intelligence, and studies.

Of the many acts of love that I could tell about my grandmother, América Pérez, for me, the most significant was the entry into the family of Zoila Sánchez del Risco. They said that one day, a chubby and shy girl of about twelve years old knocked on the door of the house and asked for something to eat. These were difficult times in the home economy: people were experiencing the crisis of Machado's presidency. The only thing my grandmother could share with her was a piece of bread with sausage and coffee. They say that she ate it with great pleasure, and at the end, she told my grandmother: "I want to help you by cleaning your house; please, let me." My grandmother refused and bid her farewell with affection. Zoila, who was nicknamed Manine at home, returned the next day: "Madam, I'm not here to ask you anything, but you have been so good that I want to help you with something...". My grandmother decided to find out about Zoila's life and discovered that she had lost her mother about two years before, that her father had abandoned her and her siblings, and that her eldest sister, Luz, was busy taking care of three male brothers and a sister the best she could. With the full agreement of her older sister, Manine came to live with my family and became an extremely beloved character for us. I have said many times that she was an angel of the Lord in the family.

As a result of an accident during a hurricane when she was a child and her family's neglect, a nail got stuck in her head, and they say this caused her an intellectual disability. Those who knew her superficially did not realize it, but Manine was never able to learn to read and write, even though everyone in our family tried to teach her. She learned to call by phone, but only to some numbers that she was very clear about. She could do some simple math, but sometimes she was cheated on purchases.

God gave my wife Ormara and me the privilege of caring for her and giving her all the love she deserved until the moment the Lord called her into his presence.

Although Manine accompanied my grandmother to church as a teenager and young woman, she never made a profession of faith. She felt herself to be a Roman Catholic, she venerated the Virgin of Charity of Cobre and attended mass on certain days of obligation. The new understanding of the faith that she acquired, from an evangelical-Protestant perspective, occurred in her adult life, especially when she lived with us in Ciego de Ávila. I did not have the privilege of baptizing her. When she received baptism, I was not ordained to the Holy Ministry. She was accompanied, among others, by Carmen Barreto, Rafael Almeida, and Pablo Ulloa, the first to be baptized at the Emmanuel Baptist Church.

I am, therefore, a difficult-to-classify mixture of two very dissimilar families who developed in an extremely complicated time for the formation of personality.

The Intermediates

The Baptist churches affiliated with the Eastern Convention had various areas of work. There was none of them that did not house the Women's Missionary Society within it.

Women carried out extensive work characterized by missionary work. The program of the so-called missionary talents was also significant. They used their gifts to support local and even denominational work. Not all churches had the Society of Knights, which was a late implant in the Convention. This area of work was almost non-existent before the 1950s.

For its part, the work with youth was very well organized, to such an extent that the Federation of Young Baptists was established throughout the territory of the provinces that made up the Convention – Camagüey and Oriente. This, although it was an organization of the Convention, had a certain autonomy and a seat on its board of directors.

Within the scope of what was the Youth Federation, which was later called the Youth Convention, there was work with adolescents, but not work with single young women, which functioned, although not widespread in the conventional area, under the denomination of World Brotherhood of Young Ladies (HMS). This work was guided by the Women's Missionary Societies of each church.

Living According to the Circumstances

The teenagers gathered around what was called the Intermediate Baptist Union. Girls and boys from twelve to sixteen or seventeen years old participated. It was a very dynamic and enthusiastic group in the churches where it was organized. To articulate their work at the level of the Convention, the youth appointed a general councilor, a position that was later called conventional promoter of work with youth.

In the First Baptist Church of Camagüey, the Union of Intermediates was felt by its well-defined group of members and the dynamics of its action. I knew about its existence since I was part of the primary school class (eight to twelve years old) that Sister Conchita Escalante taught in Sunday School. I dreamed of being part of that active group that carried out such attractive activities, but my age did not allow it. At that time, the advisor of the intermediates was Sister Febe Abella Selva, from Baracoa, who was studying teaching at the Normal School for Teachers of Camagüey and lived in the pastoral house. It was very common for girls from the eastern province or from the province of Camagüey itself to rent spaces in the pastoral house to study at the Normal School. The pastor's wife, Consuelo Sánchez Paneque, managed to take care of her eight children and those additional guests, who, thanks to the financial resources they contributed, made the family's economy more bearable.

Living According to the Circumstances

I admired Febe for her friendliness and dynamism. I attended an activity of the Intermediate Union for the first time when I was ten years old: it was a special event to say goodbye to Febe, who had finished her studies in Camagüey. I remember that it was very emotional: the president of the Union, Rubén Gregorich, gave her flowers, and there were very heartfelt words from Marirene García Mellado. I felt very close to the feelings expressed by the intermediates. I seemed to be part of the group.

About two months later, I traveled with them, all, of course, older than me, to the retreat that would be held at the El Cristo International Schools near Santiago de Cuba. Every year, summer retreats for intermediates, young people and women were held at that educational institution.

From Camagüey, people traveled on the central train, which made a stop at the El Cristo station precisely so that those who had been joining their journey from Jatibonico to that beautiful place could get off.

Participating in my first intermediate retreat was a blessing beyond what I could have expected, but it was also the first time I had traveled out of the city without the company of my parents. They accompanied me to the railway station and entrusted me to the care of Rubén Gregorich, who served as leader of the group. I have vivid memories of that retreat. The Reverend Orlando Perdomo, then a student at the seminary, gave us Bible classes under the title Interviews with Jesus. The Reverend Dante Sánchez told us about the founder of the Boy Scouts, a topic in which he was a specialist. Sister Ena Maristany gave a wonderful course in which she showed us famous paintings related to the life of the Lord Jesus Christ, and she invited us to describe them and talk about their content.

I liked the morning and evening services. We did the first ones under the trees with the girls and the second ones in front of the building dedicated to the boys' dormitory without the girls being present. The excursion to a river, exactly next to the bridge where the central train crossed and surrounded by a huge forest of wild reeds, was unforgettable. There, we were surprised by a heavy downpour, and since I had never been allowed to bathe in the rain, I greatly enjoyed that forbidden "adventure." The climax of the retreat was the consecration bonfire, one of those activities that fills your intellect and feelings and, furthermore, due to the way it was conducted, appealed to decision-making. I believe that it was, even without saying it publicly or secretly, the moment of my decision for Jesus Christ.

Upon returning from El Cristo, I was part of those who gave testimony in the church and, of course, I stayed in the Union of Intermediates of the First Baptist Church of Camagüey.

In September of that year, 1952, Dr. Gloria García Mellado assumed the responsibility of being the advisor of the intermediates, and Rubén Gregorich continued with his task of presiding over it, even though, due to his age, he should have become part of the Youth Union. Dr. García Mellado was a Physics professor at the Secondary Education Institute of Camagüey. She had been the first woman to graduate from the University of Havana with a doctorate in Physics-Mathematics Sciences. She was apparently strong and imposing but, in reality, sweet and affectionate.

The students at the Institute feared her because of her level of demands, but they said that she was an excellent teacher. In the church, in addition to being a counselor for the intermediates, she was one of the pianists and the director of the choir, from which she demanded discipline as severe as from her students.

In the elections at the end of the year, Rubén said goodbye to the group, and we elected his brother, Juan Enrique Gregorich, as president, nine months older than me but who was much ahead of me in maturity and ability. I, of course, dreamed of being the leader of the group.

For several years, Quique, as we called Juan Enrique, was the president of the Union of Intermediates, and I was its vice president. That situation changed when he began his high school studies. Quique got involved immediately in the student struggles against the dictatorship of Fulgencio Batista, which took up much of his free time. He did not stop being an integral part of the intermediate group or fulfilling his duties in the First Church, but the activities at the Institute took up a lot of his time. I believe I was president of the Union for three consecutive years.

Dr. Gloria García Mellado, as a counselor, was followed by several people who took on this complex but beautiful job of spiritually guiding the teenagers of the church. Among them, I especially remember brothers Arquímedes del Risco and Margot Lamadrid. Stability in this work was achieved when Sister Lucy Nieves Ramírez assumed responsibility for it. From the beginning, we welcomed Lucy, young, friendly, expressive and affectionate, who won the affection of the group. Every Saturday at four in the afternoon, we met to carry out the program that we had previously planned. I remember that we organized the activities by quarter. I would go to her house, and there, we would make plans that we would then carry out.

We learned a lot from Lucy; she was, in every sense of the word, a great guide. Her concern for us was comprehensive: she encouraged us to study, to participate in the life of the church, to increase our devotional life, to cultivate education, and to increase culture. There was no sphere of human endeavor in which she did not intervene for our formation. I believe that I owe much of who I am in the life of faith to my "counselor," Lucy Nieves.

Living According to the Circumstances

From that group of intermediates, at least two pastors emerged: Ángela María Hernández Gutiérrez, from the Getsemaní Baptist Church of Camagüey, and I, but also someone who, without being an active pastor, has spiritually guided hundreds of people: Nancy Guerra Pérez. The seed planted in the Union of Intermediates has borne fruit in one way or another in the lives of those of us who have passed through there. I arrived at the age at which I should no longer continue in the group, and it was then that Lucy asked me to replace her in the role of Union advisor.

Needless to say, although I believed it was more than I could do, I gladly accepted. The girls and boys who were under my guidance gave me a lot of joy and required me to deepen my knowledge of the psychological characteristics of adolescents in order to understand them. I remember a phrase from Sister Noema Carracedo, mother of two of those intermediates: "Noel is the pastor of these boys." I felt very proud.

Arquímedes del Risco Alard, his sisters Marta and Deborah, Marta and Abraham Proveyer, Jezabel Comas, Engracita Álvarez, Guillermo del Risco, Maritza Montejo, Estanila Hernández, Justo Senate, Nancy and Bernardo Díaz, Eunice and Lidia Castro, Pepe and Marilú Pau, Carlos Albornoz, Maribel and Marisol Aguilar, Benjamín and Ángela Rosell,

Lucrecia Martínez and, most especially, Leanisia Martínez, are names and figures that are indelible in my memories.

In 1965, shortly after Ormara and I were married, we were appointed counselors or promoters of work with the intermediates in the Baptist Convention of Eastern Cuba. It was an undeserved privilege for us, and for four years, we carried out that work.

Every year we prepared a program of activities to carry out, that we sent to the churches where the group existed. We also sent a devotional guide to use when the adolescents went to a school in the countryside. I wrote one of those annual activity brochures while I was in a Military Production Assistance Unit (UMAP).

Unfortunately, we were relieved of that responsibility due to the criticism made by a sister, very valuable indeed, but with an extremely conservative and not at all ecumenical position, who disagreed with one of the programs contained in the brochure and she made it known at a meeting of the Board of Directors of the Convention. It was the suggestion of carrying out a program under the title of Via Crucis, which consisted of placing some illustrative plates of the experiences lived by the Lord on the way to Calvary and standing in front of them, reading the corresponding biblical passage, commenting on it, praying and singing. That same sister, who then censored us, was years later a member of a commission of the Council of Churches of

Cuba called Semillas de Esperanza, in which she was my closest collaborator.

As part of our responsibility with the work of the youth, as those who were previously intermediate continued to be called in the conventional media, Ormara and I assumed the direction of the Youth Retreats at the Villa Teresita facilities, the Activities Camp of the Eastern Convention, in Céspedes, Camagüey.

The first of these events, our litmus test, was inspiring because of the interest that the participants showed in what they were being taught, because of the dynamism in the activities carried out, and because of their discipline, but the second camp was the climax of these events. The Convention of the former province of Oriente was not granted the permission required at that time for this type of activity, which caused a large group of girls and boys to come from Las Tunas, Palma Soriano, Moa, and Santiago de Cuba. Pastor Asael Corrales had to bring those from Palma Soriano. How restless those youths were! It seemed as if they had learned the dynamism of Reverend Corrales, then a student at the Baptist Theological Seminary of Santiago de Cuba. Those from Santiago de Cuba arrived accompanied by Ismary and Ester Oro, leaders of the First Baptist Church of that city. It is pleasant to remember the tremendous cooperation of both in the development of that retreat.

Living According to the Circumstances

Of course, the huge group of cities mentioned above overflowed the capabilities of the Villa. I had to sleep on a dining room table!

I remember the course that Nancy Guerra taught: Living the Christian Faith to the Full. I do not forget Sister Rogelita Alemany, also a student at the Baptist Theological Seminary of Santiago de Cuba, who later became the wife of the Reverend Roy Acosta and who, with the sympathy that characterized her and still characterizes her, won the affection of the participants. She managed to unite the efforts of groups formed with the objective of washing the dishes in the dining room: "Smiling is very easy to do, it gives immense pleasure to smile, smile everywhere..." and, while they "smiled", the plates, the glasses, and the cauldrons were clean and well organized.

There were only three experiences of this nature. After saying goodbye to this responsibility in the Eastern Convention, we never again had the privilege of serving in any of its areas, something we have regretted all our lives.

When we moved to Ciego de Ávila in 1968, the first thing I did at the First Baptist Church was to reorganize the Intermediate Union. Surprisingly, the group we managed to gather there was larger than the one we had had in Camagüey.

Every Saturday at four in the afternoon we met and developed a program appropriate to their interests and characteristics. The contradictions between the work of the church and civic duty that arose in the sixties in our country and increased in the following decade undermined that work; some non-Christian parents withdrew their children from the group, a few families integrated into the church spaced out their presence, and the group became very weak. But what determined the end of that precious work was the incomprehension of a mother, a member of the church, who requested my dismissal as a Sunday School teacher for teenagers.

As I narrate in the chapter dedicated to my teaching vocation, she read on the blackboard of the classroom where she taught on Sundays a thought by Ernesto "Che" Guevara, which said: "The day that Christians are capable of giving a comprehensive testimony of their faith, the Latin American revolution will be invincible." That day's class focused on Christian testimony, and I conceived it based on Che's expression. I think it was a lot to ask for that church, but the students present –Robertico Morgado, Danielito Gómez, Rafael Cepero, Sarah Pérez, Loida Hernández, Loidita López, Magaly Hernández, Miguel Baña, Gilbertico Hernández, Manolito Oliva, Cándido Alonso, Roberto Portilla, Magdiel de la Rosa and others – actively participated in the analysis and discussion of the proposed topic.

Living According to the Circumstances

The pastor of the church, the Reverend Melvin Puebla Rodríguez, called me that same day, and even without a collective decision, my work with adolescents and my teaching in that church ended forever.

One of my unforgettable memories related to the intermediates is that Ormara and I met at a Retreat of Intermediates in July 1957.

In the same place, and in a Confraternity of Intermediates that we organized from Camagüey, we coincided, or rather we convened, and sitting under one of the local coconut trees, we became engaged in June of the following year. I think we celebrated it by participating in the most popular of the dances of that time in our activities: "Thief, thief, his name is, he has stolen my little friend, but soon I will find a much prettier one."

Living According to the Circumstances

Teaching Vocation

Since I was a child, I showed interest in being a teacher. I remember that, in the summer, at least during part of the three months of vacation that primary school students then enjoyed, I was enrolled in a Review at the little school of María del Carmen Álvarez, an empirical teacher who, in the very narrow space of the living room of her house on Carmen Street, where she brought together boys of all ages from the neighborhood.

When I was in sixth grade in the summer of 1953, she "hired" me to teach the second-grade boys, whom she gathered on a back porch. I really liked the idea, and for two months, instead of receiving the review, as they assumed in my house, I taught classes to the second-grade children. I did not receive any remuneration, except that I could snack on what the teacher sold during recess. It was my first experience as an educator.

In the summer of 1956, I enrolled in a preparation course for the entrance exams at the Professional School of Commerce and/or the Normal School of Teachers. My aspiration was to obtain a place in the second, not the first one. My family was alarmed, they did not want me to study teaching in any way. Everyone at home agreed that I should study commerce to become a professional accountant. The entrance exams at the Professional School of Commerce were before those at the Teachers' Normal School, and without having made an excessive effort, I managed to obtain the number fifteen in a ranking of more than four hundred applicants, which gave me certain entry into said institution. My parents believed that I should not take entrance exams at the Normal School. After all, they said, "You should become an accountant, which does not involve the efforts of a teacher." That's how I ended up at the Professional School of Commerce of Camagüey and not at the Normal School of Teachers, much less at the Baptist Seminary, which some members of the church encouraged me to do, claiming that I had a vocation as a pastor.

The student struggles against the dictatorship of Fulgencio Batista, characterized, among other things, by frequent student strikes, caused my parents to remove me from that campus and enroll me in Colegio Pinson, an institution of the Methodist Church, to continue my studies of accounting and, at the same time, take a bilingual secretarial course, which I was able to complete. I also took advantage of the time to enroll in high school. Some subjects were common, so they could be done with some ease.

The triumph of the Revolution came while I was in my second year of accounting and high school. The revolutionary hustle and bustle, the multiple activities that political change entailed, fascinated me, and with difficulty, I managed to finish the third year of studies at Pinson. In the middle of that course, in May 1960, they made me the offer to start working as a teacher in the Rebel Army. I accepted because it involved giving night classes at the old Monteagudo Barracks. A month and a half later, classes became daytime, but fortunately, the course at Pinson had already concluded.

Since mid-June of that year, I became a teacher in the Instruction Department of the Revolutionary Armed Forces. I first worked as a garrison teacher at the Camagüey prison and, at the same time, in one of the three classrooms that existed on the shooting range, very close to the then Country Club and close to the Hunters Club.

I was transferred from those two places at the beginning of 1961 to give classes to the Army Corps officers in the Military Unit that was located at the back of the Camagüey airport. The classroom where I worked was exactly next to the headquarters, where Papito Serguera served as commander. The group of officers, all older than me, were in the sixth grade under my guidance.

Among the students were two captains of many combat merits named Ochoa, one of whom, Arnaldo, was later shot, despite being a Hero of the Republic of Cuba, for improper activities during the war in Angola. I do not have pleasant memories of him because his behavior was very inappropriate in the classroom. On one occasion, Commander Serguera himself had to call him out.

Living According to the Circumstances

The need to work on the Literacy Campaign made all of us teachers who worked in the Rebel Army concentrate on what was previously the Camagüey Livestock Fair, and we assumed the responsibility of teaching the rebel soldiers who had not yet learned to read and write. The classroom assigned to me had twenty-one rebel soldiers, of whom I managed to teach nineteen to read and write. Raúl Mayo and Emilio Fernández were unable to learn, which I found disconcerting and frustrating, even though neither of them had managed to learn with the other teachers at the school.

At the beginning of the 1962-1963 academic year, I knew of the need for an English teacher at the Ramón Pereda Pulgares Rural Secondary School in Cascorro, which later changed its name to Inti Peredo, and I opted for the position. I worked there as an English teacher and secretary, an activity that I began three months after arriving at that study center until almost completing the 1965-1966 academic year in which I was recruited for the Military Units to Aid Production (UMAP) on July 4, 1966.

I don't think I ever had, before or after, a job that fulfilled me more than the one I held at that school, where, due to certain circumstances, I had to teach Geography for a full term. In May of the same year that I was recruited for the UMAP, I was selected as a National Vanguard of Secondary Education. In March of the same year, the provincial advisor for English language teaching in the Directorate of Higher Secondary Education, Dr. Silvia López Trigo Garay, offered me the possibility of taking care of consulting in the western part of the province, that is, the territory currently occupied by the province of Ciego de Ávila. I accepted the proposal "with fear and trembling."

When Sylvia presented the proposal, the provincial director of Education, Juan Costo Navas, asked her: "Don't you have another person with more political integration than that teacher?" Dr. López Trigo was forced to propose another person who, according to her, did not meet the pedagogical conditions that she had seen in me.

At the time of being recruited to the UMAP I had managed to climb to the last of the salary tridents that were awarded to a General Secondary Education teacher. When I went on leave, I went to the Provincial Directorate of Education to request my reintegration into the classroom from which I had left, but I was denied that possibility. I then got an interview with the provincial director of Education, who told me emphatically: "You cannot work in education or as a janitor." After a few years, I found out that he had changed his residence to Miami while I was still in Cuba.

The frustrating idea of not being able to work in teaching made me very sad, but I had to look for a job. I went to the Ministry of Labor in Camagüey to request it. There, they told me that I could only work in agriculture or construction. I hit twice on the desk of the person who told me this and answered: "I haven't studied for that," to which he replied: "Well, if you refuse to accept our offer, you will be declared lazy, and the Anti-Vagrant Law will be applied to you."

My brother, an honest communist militant, was very mortified by my inability to get a job suitable to my abilities and spoke with a Party leader in the province whom I never met. He managed to insert me into a newly created classroom at the Tula Aguilera Primary School in Las Mercedes neighborhood in Camagüey, where they needed a teacher for the sixth grade, which they had not filled. I worked there for three months without a salary. The educational authorities refused to sign my appointment. I never knew why. After that time, they summoned me to Municipal Education and gave me an official appointment. I felt very fulfilled at that school. We had a good director who felt very happy with my work, but for multiple reasons, such as the rejection of some friends and family for having been a "UMAP soldier" and some hints that my wife received at the Provincial Library, where she worked, we decided to move to Ciego de Ávila.

I began the 1968-1969 school year in a fifth-grade classroom at the Eduardo R. Chibás Elementary School. On the second day, the municipal advisor, Ester Lago, visited the campus, and she summoned me to the school office with a form that I had filled out upon entering the campus. The form asked, among other things, if I had religious beliefs and of what kind, if I attended church, and if I had responsibilities there. Of course, I had answered truthfully.

The official asked me, "Was this form filled out by you? Is everything that appears in it true?" To my affirmative answer, she expressed, "We cannot accept you as a teacher in Ciego de Ávila; if you could be a teacher in Camagüey, here you can't." She didn't finish telling me those words, and I didn't finish getting up from the chair where I was sitting while I was hearing those words.

Then she very calmly told me, "Please sit down, speaking, we can understand each other." She took out a new blank form from her folder and offered it to me, saying, "Please sign this new form, we'll take care of filling it out."

That outraged me, and I responded, "Coercion, in my free judgment, I do not accept from you or from anyone. If you want me as a teacher, accept me with all my principles," saying that, I left the office to my classroom to collect my belongings and then left the school.

The director, a beautiful person, prevented me from doing so by telling me, "Don't worry, we are going to resolve the matter, please continue teaching."

Living According to the Circumstances

I finished the course, and the next year, 1969-1970, I went on to work with two sixth-grade classrooms at the Alfredo Álvarez Mola school. The work at that school was exhausting, double sessions, and at night, there were mobilizations, to which I went very frequently, to fill polyethylene bags to plant coffee plants in the nursery that was located on the Ciego de Ávila highway to the Venezuela sugar mill. On Saturdays, we had courses in which I generally taught Mathematics to the other teachers.

At the beginning of the 1971-1972 school year, I went to work as an English teacher at the Sugar Technical School in the Venezuela sugar mill. The following year, the local Workers' Peasant Faculty was organized, and I first became a mathematics teacher and later worked, at the same time, as director and received the same salary.

In a mobilization for agriculture in which we worked in cultural attention to sugar cane in the vicinity of Gato Prieto, the Communist Youth of the Ciego de Ávila region was to mobilize us "due to an imperative need for the harvest" to work in the sugarcane plantations of central Haiti, in Santa Cruz del Sur. The camp to which we were transferred did not meet the minimum conditions to house us. For two nights, we slept on the ground, and we barely had water for the most urgent needs. I warned the head of the camp that if the conditions did not exist, the students of the faculty he directed would not go to work.

Sleeping on the floor, no one can handle a job as difficult as the one we have here. This greatly bothered the boss, who sent for the leaders of the Communist Youth of the province. They came to discuss with me and the first thing they asked me was, "Are you a member of the Party?"

When I answered no, a second question came. "And are you a member of the Communist Youth?"

Upon my second refusal, they told me that they had nothing to discuss with me and turned their backs on me.

Very mortified, I told them, "If you have nothing to discuss with me, I will go with my students to the same place where they brought us, where there is enough work for everyone," and we left.

Of course, two days later, they sent a new director of the faculty to the Gato Prieto camp, and three months later, they fired me from my position as a Mathematics teacher on that campus. I was never again able to give free rein in the secular sphere to my teaching vocation.

In the religious field, I began to teach at the Sunday Bible School in the Piedra Imán mission of the First Baptist Church of Camagüey, where I had responsibilities since I was fourteen years old. One of them was the children's class every Sunday, under the accurate guidance of my "counselor," Lucy Nieves. I remember that in the First Baptist Church of Camagüey, we teenagers participated in the Heralds of the King class, which Sister Cruz María Bermúdez taught with great dedication every Sunday. We left it at the age of sixteen, the boys to the Berean class, whose teacher was brother Rafael Gregorich Sánchez, and the girls to the Dorcas class, of which Dr. Aurelia Barrios was the teacher. I had no interest in going to the class that Brother Gregorich taught, even though I recognized that he was very good at teaching the Bible.

Together with others in the group, we encouraged the idea of creating a high school class, as it was called, which would house those of us who, from the ages of sixteen to nineteen, still considered ourselves full-fledged adolescents. Several teachers passed through it, none of them adjusted to the group, we were not easy at all.

Boldly, I took on the role of class teacher, I think against the opinion of the elders. Since then, at less than seventeen years old, and practically to this day, I have carried out the beautiful task of teaching the Bible to different groups in the churches where I have been.

However, in September 1977, I was fired from my responsibility as a teacher at the Sunday Bible School of the First Baptist Church of Ciego de Ávila.

At that moment, like so many times, I taught classes to teenagers, a large group interested in learning. My separation was motivated by the protest of a mother who saw written on the blackboard a phrase by Ernesto Guevara, with whose analysis and discussion concluded that day the teaching on the integrity of Christian testimony.

I think that the experience I had on the Sunday following being separated from my responsibility as a teacher of adolescents in that congregation, together with the fact that I had also previously been separated from my responsibility as a Mathematics teacher, made that the saddest Sunday of my life. I decided not to go to church, I stayed at home washing clothes and ruminating on my sadness. It was a long, silent, and reflective morning.

I always proposed what I repeated on occasions to friends, "I will return to be a teacher in this country, I will return to the classroom one day, this situation has to change." The loss of sight prevented me from achieving that dream, which became possible in Cuba after the changes that occurred since the early 1990s.

My situation was not an isolated event: hundreds of teachers and professors were separated from the classrooms for our Christian convictions. I remember so many colleagues, I think all of them with a vocation for teaching, were adequately prepared, and most importantly, with a formal education that they transmitted to their students.

Living According to the Circumstances

A vivid example was what happened at the Cascorro school, from which I left for the UMAP. Several valuable colleagues remained working there. Two of them, Roberto Cruz Legrá, professor of Physics, and Sergio Martínez Pozo, professor of Chemistry, were part of the same congregation as me at the First Baptist Church of Camagüey. One morning, unexpectedly, without prior announcement, the municipal director of Education of Guáimaro and the secretary of the Education Sector core appeared at the school, gathered the director, the secretary of the school's Communist Party core, and four teachers - the two mentioned previously and those of Geography and Spanish – to tell them that they were separated from their positions as teachers for "not contributing to the formation of the new man."

The municipal director of Education asked if any of the four had anything to say. Roberto Cruz raised his hand and when they gave him the floor, he expressed, "I don't understand what you mean by forming the new man. We, and I in particular, have collaborated in everything that the center has requested, and I have given of my free time to promote culture and knowledge."

Subsequently, Sergio was placed as a worker at the Vertientes sugar mill, and Roberto, who left the country two years later, worked in the office of the Camagüey Railway Company.

I believe that from that unjustified action, the educational process in the country began to break down. There were no role models for the new generations, teachers were improvised, and the sad thing about the improvisation was not the lack of academic preparation of the new ones, but rather the use of people who had no love for teaching and who were not what they should be, "a living Gospel."

When, in March 2004, I was invited to join the Chair of Disability Studies at the Faculty of Psychology of the University of Havana, I took a deep breath and raised my prayer of gratitude to the Lord. I did not return to teaching in its traditional form, to which I had aspired, but through another training pathway. The Chair gave me the opportunity to attend, more than once, conferences, presentations, and debates on various topics, all related to disability, but which were undoubtedly ways of educational training.

On the other hand, the effort to include the issue of disability in the theological institutions of Cuba and Latin America also became a channel of my vocation for teaching. Nearly fifteen Spanish-speaking theological institutions have given me the joy of teaching.

For me, this has been God's answer to my prayers and the reward for my sustained vocation. I lack systematic theological training in a seminary. I have only attended courses, workshops, and conferences, and I have a lifetime of experience in Cuban and Latin American Christian work.

The fact that someone with these characteristics could share a professorship in theological institutions of all kinds is, simply, the mercy of God with a person who was born to teach.

Living According to the Circumstances

Forced To Be An Accountant

As I have already said, my vocation for teaching was visible since my primary education, but my elders almost forced me to become an accountant. Their concern was understandable. A graduate of the Normal School for Teachers entered a ladder in which political favoritism prevailed, he/she had to start in a rural school, and getting to work in a primary school in the city took years.

On the other hand, working in a private school meant, in addition to many recommendations, a lower salary. Private schools almost always pay fifty percent less than a classroom in the public sector. In addition to the fact that a professional accountant earned more, the jobs were in the city and provided better conditions for further study.

Entering the Professional School of Commerce, like any other state study center of Secondary Professional Education, was extremely complicated. These institutions made calls every year to cover a number of places much smaller than the existing demand.

For the selection process, entrance exams were taken to which one was entitled after paying the admission fee. Safe places were available, of course, to those who enjoyed the support of some influential person in politics or in the administration of the institution to which they aspired. The most intelligent and/or studious managed to enter the center, but many who could have entered were left out.

I was not one of the most talented ones, so they enrolled me in an academy located in the La Vigía neighborhood of Camagüey to prepare me for admission. I was encouraged by the fact that this preparatory course could also be used to pass the admission exam at the Normal School of Teachers. The preparatory course was very good. All the teachers were very capable and interested in their work.

The admission exam for the Professional School of Commerce was usually held a few days before the Normal School, so I thought that if I didn't get a place in the first one, I would try for the second one.

My cousin Ricardo Guzmán, Pupy, was preparing for admission with me, who would also choose to enter the School of Commerce, although, to tell the truth, he was not very interested in it either, his vocation was mechanics. But in the house, it was considered inadmissible for him to spend the whole day "getting covered in oil".

The day of the entrance tests arrived, and among more than four hundred applicants, we got a place, although I suspect that recommendations were involved, which they never confessed to us. Passing the exam deeply pleased my entire family, who encouraged me to the point of exhaustion to accept what I had achieved. They refused to let me take the entrance tests for the normal school, which would mean a new outlay.

"Why are you going to go through that nervousness if you already have a secure place?" my mother asked me.

So, I started accounting studies. I didn't feel bad during the first course, which they called pre-commercial. It was 1956, and the student class expressed, in many ways, its disagreement with the Batista dictatorship. The Student Association, which I joined as soon as the course began, was a hive of censure and protests against the abuses of the dictatorship. The Geography teacher, very qualified, did not enjoy the support of the Student Association, which accused her of being a "finger teacher," which meant that she had acquired the position without having submitted to the call. Due to her ties with officials of the dictatorship, they had put her in that job, violating the ranks.

The Student Association protested. I participated in the meeting in which the protest was prepared and also in the meeting with the faculty. The meeting concluded with threats from the director, who accused the Association of boycotting the center's educational process instead of supporting teaching. The confrontation was so strong that we "gave up" and stayed with the teacher, with whom we did not sympathize despite the quality of her classes.

Living According to the Circumstances

The following year, when I was in my first year, the situation became much more belligerent. On more than one occasion, the students declared a strike. One of them was violently interrupted. When we left, a patrol car approached, and some received blows from the police. I finished the course, but my parents decided that I should continue my accounting studies at a private institution that was partially exempt from student struggles.

That's how I returned to Pinson School. Accounting studies at Pinson had a different focus, and the fact that all the teachers were young and very close to the students, in addition to the good friends I acquired there, encouraged me to study a career that interested me.

I completed the bilingual secretarial course, which was two years long, and continued my accounting studies until the school was nationalized in 1961. The 1960-1961 academic year was very irregular. I was already immersed in the work of a teacher in the Rebel Army, and classes were suspended so that literacy campaigns held in the country could be encouraged. I didn't finish the course.

At the beginning of 1962, after the Literacy Campaign, I returned to the Professional School of Commerce and graduated as an accountant-planner in 1963.

Living According to the Circumstances

I kept the title and continued in my teaching work, but I had to dust it off in 1972 when I was separated from the teaching profession for the second time. At first, I didn't need it, because they placed me as an office worker in the Human Resources Department at the Venezuela sugar mill. There I worked, more than anything else, as a typist with the director of Human Resources, Dagoberto Plasencia Pámenes, who, aware of the situation that had brought me there and my commitment to faith, went to extremes to complicate my work life. He demanded more from me than from others and assigned me extra tasks outside of work hours that affected my religious participation. They put a phrase in very large print on my employment file: RELIGIOUS PROBLEMS. It was a warning to everyone, and especially to future employers.

I wanted to leave this job quickly. It was more than fifteen kilometers from my home, they only paid me one hundred pesos a month, and I had to work a tiring eight-hour schedule. Some of my colleagues treated me with kindness and appreciated the harshness of my boss's treatment of me. One of them, with whom I related the most, named Blanco, encouraged me to look for another job.

During my first vacation, I started looking for work in Ciego de Ávila. There were three centers that were enthusiastic about the presentation I gave them, "I am an accountant-planner graduated from the Camagüey Business School, although I have no experience working as an accountant, and I also have a secretary's degree...". The first two places told me that they had to make certain inquiries and would give me an answer the next day.

Both gave me identical answers, "We deeply regret not being able to give you the accountant position. When we found out, we learned that the granting of new places is currently frozen."

In the third place – the Regional Health Directorate of Ciego de Ávila – it was different. They had made arrangements and, recommended by someone, they accepted me. The director of the Economic Department appreciated me and instructed me, but before the end of my first week, they called me to the Human Resources Department and told me that I could not take the accountant position that they had promised me and that, instead, they offered me a position as an office worker B in the maintenance workshop of the MINSAP Regional Directorate. I accepted. There, the salary would be one hundred pesos, but I needed to work. I worked in that place for almost a year. The work was done in about two hours of the morning shift. I had plenty of time the rest of the time, but I had to stay in the center. That allowed me to read a lot. I could think, like the sacred writer, that "everything works for good."

A co-worker of Ormara at the Public Library, who, for many reasons, we will never forget, Carmen Barreto, a Party activist, and a true revolutionary, did not agree with the marginalization to which I was subjected and offered to get me an interview with Mr. Albadio Pérez, who at the time was addressing the economic issue in the Regional Party.

One night, I went to the interview with Albadio, who listened to my story with careful politeness and visible interest, and he offered me help. Thanks to his intervention, I started working as an accounting assistant at the Seed Company. The director of the Economic Area was José Rodríguez, someone who knew how to lead and who put me under the guidance of the company's accountant so that I could learn in practice what I had acquired in theory. I think that's where I became an accountant.

I then went on to work as the main accountant at the Higher Agricultural Institute of Ciego de Ávila (ISACA), which was a disaster as far as economic controls were concerned.

When I arrived a few months before, it had been separated from the University of Camagüey and established direct links with the Ministry of Higher Education, but in relation to the economic area, nothing had been disaggregated, organized, or put under precise controls. We had to start from scratch.

I felt challenged by the work of the institution, and even more so because the economic vice-rector, a colleague from Havana named Bocourt, wanted, and his work demonstrated it, to organize the disaster we had inherited. I felt fully supported by that colleague, and together, we began to establish the required controls. It was not easy, we organized an area, and when we turned our backs, everything returned to the previous situation, and not precisely due to inability, but due to personal convenience.

Another difficulty in carrying out my job was my immediate bosses. One of them had acquired the twelfth grade in courses at the Peasant Worker Faculty, and judging by his poor use of the language and his misspellings, it seemed that it had been given to him as a gift. Of course, he knew nothing about economic controls. The other was not interested in his work, he lived in Morón and could never stay outside of work hours, no matter how long it was, because "in which means of transportation am I going to leave next?"

I, however, on one occasion, had to stay all night making and reviewing payroll for the next day's payment because there was no one in the area who could do it. My two immediate bosses were Party members and, therefore, completely trusted people at the institute. I, on the other hand, only had the sympathies and support of the vice-rector of the Economy.

The excess of responsibilities and the ineffectiveness of my work due to the existing disorder forced me to leave the ISACA, and I returned to the Seed Company to occupy the position of accountant. I was in that role for a while, and I felt fulfilled because I was finally able to put into practice what I had studied. The then head of the economic area was very demanding but a capable executive. He always supported me and provided me with all the facilities to carry out my duties.

At that time, they approached me on two occasions to propose my inclusion in the ranks of the Party as long as I abandoned my Christian faith. The two people who interviewed me argued with my position on life, work and the Revolution, but... of course, I maintained my points of view and my convictions.

With more knowledge of accounting, but without liking what I did, I went to work to improve my salary at EXPEDITRAN, a company of the Ministry of Transportation, as a specialist in accounting and costs. The boss was a colleague who had worked with me during my first time at the Seed Company. From a cleaning assistant – she had become literate during the Literacy Campaign – she had been promoted to cashier because of her intelligence, she showed lively signs of interest and stood out for the quality of her work. Already working with us, she took the middle technical course in Accounting, and years later, she studied for a degree in Economics. As director of the economic area of EXPEDITRAN, she invited me to go work with her and I accepted.

My work in this entity was more technical, but overwhelmingly boring, always the same. The group was good, but the boss's character gradually soured and became more and more authoritarian. The simplicity and affability that had characterized her vanished, and her despotic nature unfortunately surfaced.

The "martyrdom" that it meant for me to be sitting behind a bureau surrounded by official documents, controls, and numbers concluded in EXPEDITRAN when, in November 1986, a medical commission diagnosed me with a total and permanent disability, which allowed me to retire. I decided that I would never again be tied down to anything that had to do with numbers and accounting notes.

After retiring, I went to work voluntarily in the special area of the Roberto Rivas Fraga Provincial Library, where, by resolution of the Ministry of Labor, I occupied the position of technician after passing a course for that purpose.

In January 1988, we held the first Braille Readers Meeting, an event that has continued to be held. Since then, with rare exceptions for work reasons, I have been part of the organization and execution of said event.

Ideal Help

I met Ormara in July 1957. Fresh in my memory is the image of those three teenagers, Norma Díaz Rosado, Fermín León Martin and her, who arrived at Villa Teresita – the conference camp of the Baptist Convention of Eastern Cuba, located in the Céspedes power plant in the municipality of Florida in Camagüey – accompanied by Dr. Olga Montes Oquendo, counselor of the Union of Intermediates in Ciego de Ávila. For the first time, a group from Ciego de Ávila participated in the Intermediate Retreat, in which I had already been three times before.

The boys who had participated in that activity for the most years, Evelito Jardines Labrada, Joel Reyes, and I, disputed the "special friendship" of the girls, and it seemed to me that the smallest of the two who arrived could be the "piece to conquer" that summer.

In the activity there were girls and boys from other places in the former province of Camagüey and also from Las Tunas. From Florida came a brunette with light eyes named Mirna Vázquez Sosa, who also interested me. I became friends with Ormara and Mirna, and even though I was more inclined to Ciego de Ávila than to Florida, the uncertainty about which of the two I should fall in love within those days was a great

Living According to the Circumstances

dilemma. I spent much of the night in rhythmic games in pairs, sometimes with Ormara and other times with Mirna.

The activity concluded with a declaration of love to Mirna, which was reciprocated. However, upon reaching my house in Camagüey, almost immediately, I wrote to Ormara, who boldly responded to me. Ormara has never liked writing letters. I have always said that she has the gift of oral communication and not written communication, unlike me. Her mother, Alicia, was surprised to see her answering a letter: it was something very unusual.

We met again on December 7 of that year in Jatibonico. Every year the District Convention of Baptist Churches was held then, where sisters and brothers from the churches of the former province of Camagüey met.

At around noon, after having lunch, we went in a group walking to the river bridge, which was then the limit between the provinces of Camagüey and Las Villas. There, I declared my love to Ormara, who rejected me.

The correspondence between us continued, and we also had the occasional opportunity to meet, limited solely and exclusively to church activities.

In March of the following year, 1958, the intermediates from Camagüey visited those from Ciego de Ávila. I remember that it coincided with the birthday of Loida, one of Ormara's sisters.

Living According to the Circumstances

Our group's preacher was expected to be Juan Enrique Gregorich, six months older than me and the son of our church's pastor. We knew that he would preach on the conversion of the Philippian jailer, which was his usual sermon at special events or out of town.

At the last minute he could not attend for reasons of his responsibility as leader of the Student Association of the Secondary Education Institute of Camagüey, where he was studying. The counselor of the intermediates, Lucy Nieves Ramírez, asked me to preach. I had only occupied the pulpit months before at the Céspedes Baptist Church. I remember that I selected Psalm 84 for the occasion. I don't remember anything about the sketch I made, but I do remember the face of Ormara's parents, who, sitting on a bench, looked at me intently. I didn't know what Ormara's opinion was either, although years later when we were married, I discovered in her Bible the text marked with the date of that afternoon.

Our next meeting was on June 14 of that year. At the initiative of our Union of Intermediates, we would have that day in Villa Teresita a Provincial Confraternity of Intermediates. The retreats, not only for teenagers but also for women and young people, had been suspended; the rebellion against the Batista dictatorship did not recommend events of this nature. That day was marked on the calendar of our existence. Ormara accepted my love. Sitting both on a coconut tree that resembled an "L," bent by a cyclone that hit the place, a trembling but not hesitant "yes" accelerated the rhythm of my heart.

That day, Ormara returned to her house and, almost immediately, made her decision known to her mother. At that time, a more or less formal courtship at the age of sixteen in a traditional Christian setting was not something to applaud. But with the wisdom that always characterized her, my mother-in-law, instead of being scared, uncomfortable, or trying to dissuade Ormara, told her about my family.

Alicia and Mom had met as children when they were both leaders of the so-called Rayitos del Sol Society. In addition, the pastor who had baptized Mom in 1927 in Camagüey had later baptized Alicia in Ciego de Ávila. The two daughters of that pastor, the Reverend Guillermo Rodríguez, Minerva, and Isis, especially the latter, had been very close friends of both.

On the other hand, Alicia remembered with pleasure my parents' wedding held at the First Baptist Church of Ciego de Ávila, in which her sister Nena had been part of the choir.

The first months of our commitment were the last of the rebellion of the Cuban people against the disastrous dictatorship of Fulgencio Batista. It was not advisable that young people travel outside the town, and, furthermore, I spent the last four months of 1958 confined in the house of my cousin

Living According to the Circumstances

Ricardo Guzmán, Pupy, on 62 San Miguel Street. It was a preventive measure.

Being together and in the neighborhood where we had the greatest number of friends, we avoided the usual "nightlife" of young people of our age. It was a pleasant experience, but also an opportunity to contribute, within our possibilities, to the overthrow of the dictatorship. Some of our young friends were immersed in political struggles. They transported medicines and supplies for the combatants in the mountains, as well as some weapons and propaganda against the dictatorship. My parents unknowingly encouraged an activity in which they did not want to see me involved for fear of retaliation.

The dawn of January 1, 1959, brought with it, among many other things, ample opportunities to travel to Ciego de Ávila, if not every weekend. I cannot forget the first Sunday I had lunch at Ormara's house.

When I returned home, Mom asked me, "How were you treated at Alicia's house? What did they give you for lunch?"

I replied, "Rice with chicken, fried plantains, tomato salad... and surprise yourself with wine."

Mom, who was very conservative and never bathed in the sea or a river so as not to wear a bathing suit, said in amazement, "My God, how odd! Wine in a Christian family home!"

Living According to the Circumstances

Our courtship was extremely conservative, given the time and the family's Protestant tradition. We couldn't go alone even a block and a half from Ormara's house, where the temple of the First Church of Ciego de Ávila was located.

At night, when we returned from worship and while I was waiting for the bus from the Santiago-Havana company that made the Santa Clara-Holguín route and passed at 10:20 at night, Ormara and I would sit on the sofa in the living room to share our experiences and enjoy each other's company.

My good mother-in-law would sit on a small rocking chair in the adjoining dining room to review the magazine El Mensajero, the official organ of the Baptist Convention of Eastern Cuba, Sunday school lessons, and old papers in such a way that she could, to avoid the popular censure, "take care" of her little daughter.

Although I think I earned the affection of my future in-laws very early on, they did not lose the habit. I remember that, in March 1959, when we were returning from the Annual Assembly of the Baptist Convention of Eastern Cuba, held in Guantánamo in the heat of rejoicing over the recent liberation from the dictatorship, night fell, leaving Santiago de Cuba. My father-in-law sent Nidia, the youngest sister, to take the place I had on the bus next to Ormara so as to avoid the temptation of "succumbing to the darkness of the night...".

Living According to the Circumstances

We celebrated our wedding on September 12, 1965, at the First Baptist Church of Ciego de Ávila. There were seven years of courtship, interrupted for two. We decided to break up in April 1962 because misunderstandings had arisen between us. We did not agree on issues that we considered decisive for the unity of a couple. In that period, we saw each other twice.

The first, one afternoon in Camagüey, I entered the Capri cafeteria, disturbed by photophobia, which bothered me a lot. I sat down on the only empty bench, and when I realized who was on the bench on the right, I got a tremendous surprise. It was Alicia, and next to her was Ormara. I had broken up with my girlfriend and had never given an explanation to her parents, who had so kindly welcomed me into her house. Needless to say, I didn't have a snack.

I said hello, and asked what they were doing in Camagüey. I apologized and said goodbye quickly.

The other opportunity was at the Assembly of the Convention, held in Santiago de Cuba in March 1964. I was going down the stairs of the First Church with my dear friend Sergio Martínez while she went up it accompanied by her friend Dinorah Mata.

We greeted each other, and Sergio maliciously told me, "If you had noticed her loving gaze, you would have stayed talking."

Living According to the Circumstances

The conversation did not take place at that moment, but it did the next day when we agreed that I would go to Ciego de Ávila to talk. I went to her workplace, the public library, where she had worked since June 1963. There were three visits on alternate Wednesdays. That was the day that I had a meeting in the morning at the Higher Institute of Education (ISE) of Camagüey for the improvement of English teachers, which left me the rest of the day free. In the conversation on the third Wednesday, we concluded that we had resolved the difficulties that had separated us and that I should go to my father-in-law that same night to tell him about our agreement. Ormara would stay at the church Bible Study meeting while I went to her house to talk to her father.

Only his wife called my father-in-law Pepe, but in my nervousness, I greeted him with "Good night, Pepe!" I think he, instead of getting upset, smiled, and everything went well. I thank God for my father-in-law's understanding.

We prepared our wedding with great care, we wanted to do something different, and to a certain extent, we achieved it. We got married on a Sunday at seven in the morning. Some said that we would have little attendance, but that was not the case. Many people from the church, family and friends attended from Camagüey.

The previous night, I slept in the Santiago-Havana Hotel. My friend and brother Sergio Martínez accompanied me. Late in the morning, my brother arrived, who had not found a room, so we slept in the same bed. My brother was a "left-wing" communist militant. He never allowed us to buy anything on the black market at home, and in response to criticism against the revolutionary process, he came out forcefully to defend his ideals. When I told him about our marriage and told him that I would go to live in my father's house in Camagüey, where I had my room, he, who lived in his despite having his own apartment, told me, "You don't have to come to live here. I'll give you the apartment to live in."

At that time, communist militants never attended a Christian temple, and I doubted that he would go to our wedding.

When I asked him, he told me emphatically, "How do you think I'm not going to be present at your marriage?" My brother died without knowing how much I thanked him for that gesture of affection.

We invited Reverend Marino Santos Martínez, who was my wife's spiritual father, to officiate our marriage. My mother agreed to be the godmother. She looked very elegant, like my father-in-law as the godfather. Loida, Ormara's sister, was the bridesmaid whom my friend Roberto Cruz Legrá called Rebeca, evoking a famous novel by Daphne du Maurier. The boy with the rings, Danielito Gómez Daniel, and the girl with the flowers, Loidita López Bolufé, played a beautiful role. Then, they were my students in the Sunday School teen class. My father-in-law wrote a review of the ceremony that appeared in El Mensajero magazine in October of that year, and which I reproduce below:

To Ormarita at her wedding

Today, step by step, I take you by the hand, as if there was no rush to get there, towards the sanctuary where your fiancé awaits you. I contemplate your smiling face and your lost gaze forward as if you were looking at the long path that your new life has to go.

The diadem that borders your hair trembles as you walk, and the veil that covers your face trembles when you slightly tilt your head, where your young and enamored mind dreams of a world of illusion.

There is absolute silence around us, only interrupted by the wedding march that guides us towards the sanctum.

I know that hundreds of eyes look at you, and I feel happy because you are happy, but I can't stop my thoughts from going back to your earliest childhood, and I see you lying in your crib of clear whiteness, from which you look at me without even knowing me, nor knowing who I was because your few months could not appreciate the meaning of our relationships, but the Supreme Law of God united us in that filial love of parents and children.

Living According to the Circumstances

You extended your tiny arms like those of a doll towards me, and I lifted you up in mine and showered you with kisses that I placed on your rosy face.

Then you grew up, and your first word filled me with pride because the two syllables that your lips babbled were like a song to life, and since then, you never stopped pronouncing it, although, from dad, you went on to say daddy.

I took you to school in your early years, I walked you in my arms, and together, we visited the places to which opportunity took us without separating each other, always united by that filial love that is the greatest and most beautiful.

Thus, we walked the path of life as we walk this one, in which I take you to the place where you will soon find the man you love.

I'm happy because you are, but I can't stop my eyes from getting wet and I have to tighten my lips to not give vent to the emotion.

I would like to continue writing, but two salty drops have fallen on the paper and smudged the ink. There are tears held in my pupils for so long that, like a river swollen with water, it has spilled its liquid to release the greatest emotion of my life.

Living According to the Circumstances

I wish you eternal happiness.

The wedding toast was at the family home, a non-alcoholic punch, but with ginger to give it its "deceptive little touch" and a sandwich of roast pork leg with cheese. They say the cake was beautiful and delicious, I don't remember. We took everything with us in the car in which we went to Havana, but we did not know about the quality of the toast, which my father-in-law paid for, since when we arrived at the hotel, we gave it to the driver. It is worth saying that we had done the notarial wedding the day before, on September 11, in the presence of the two witnesses, Sergio Martínez Pozo and Dinorah Mata del Río.

The honeymoon was unforgettable. We spent the first days at the Habana Riviera Hotel, then we went to Soroa. We returned to the Habana Riviera to conclude at the Jagua Hotel in Cienfuegos, from where we went for a day trip to Trinidad.

The apartment that my brother had so lovingly given us consisted of a living room, dining room, kitchen, bathroom, interior patio, and a bedroom. It was located on the street of San Esteban, Oscar Primelles, almost in front of the Isla de Cuba Hotel. It was the penultimate apartment of four on the ground floor of that hallway. It was a very peaceful place, disturbed only by the neighbor at the back, who, in a loud crescendo, called her son Reinier, who was about nine years old. Our apartment became the center of activities for the youth of the First Church. Notable was the birthday party of José

Alberto Rodriguez Castelló, a Havana doctor sanctioned to work in Camagüey in an attempt to illegally leave the country. That day, without him knowing, we organized his anniversary party and received thirty-two people in that small place. Even today, I don't know how.

Our apartment was later a place of obligatory passage for pastors and seminarians recruited by the UMAP who went on a trip to Camagüey and had dinner with us, bathed, and I don't know how, wore one of my suits to go to church on Sunday night. It was inexplicable that the same suit suited everyone.

Our idyll was interrupted on July 4, 1966, nine months after the wedding, when they called me to the UMAP. If that passage in history constituted a university for me, it was also a university for Ormara. My parents tried to get her to move to her parents' house on Bembeta Street or to allow someone to accompany her at night.

From the beginning, Ormara refused to leave the apartment or have a companion. Not without a great deal of pain, loneliness, and sadness, Ormara showed courage and a great sense of the guidance of the Holy Spirit. Her life continued its normal course with the necessary maturity in the face of what was an enigma. How long would the separation last?

I believe that she earned her title of ideal help when Dr. Nelson Sosa Bada, leader of our church and specialist in otorhinolaryngology, went to visit her to tell her that the medical commission that had determined my discharge from the UMAP had come to the conclusion that I had, at most, five years of vision left. Nelson had not dared to tell me. He entrusted it to her so she could decide what to do with the news.

As soon as Ormara and I met again after I was already permanently discharged from the Military Production Assistance Unit (UMAP), she told me, "Sit down, we have to talk about something very important." There was no crying.

Ormara is not one of those women who cries easily. When she was done, it hurt me more than it had hurt her, especially since I was the cause of it. Her words and her actions were firm. God rewarded us. There were not five years that we had to prepare ourselves materially, spiritually, and culturally for the lack of sight, there were around twenty-five.

Another relevant moment of Ormara's suitability was when I decided to use a guide cane. An instructor in mobility and orientation in space from the National Association of the Blind (ANCI) suggested it to me, and she even gave me lessons on how to use it properly.

I resisted, "I don't want to give my mother the sadness of seeing her son in the same conditions in which she saw my father."

Ormara, with her wisdom and affection, encouraged me to use it, "Your mother, like me and everyone else, will feel safer knowing that you have the help of a guide cane."

I remember the afternoon I took it on the way to the post office and how, on the way back, Ormara encouraged me to continue using it. Only those of us who have needed a guide can know of its usefulness.

The cane has been very useful, but the guidance and orientation of a woman of Ormara's caliber has been the essential stimulus to fight and live.

Ormara never felt the call to the pastorate. God did not call her for that task, which does not mean that she has not been a guide and mentor to many, many people within the church or in secular life. However, when

I decided to say yes to God's call to take up the work as a pastor, Ormara encouraged me and pushed me in that direction. First, she did it with her gift as a pianist, to which she later added her ability as a driver, and in this way, her suitability grew. She was not the pastor of Emmanuel, Getsemaní, La Vid Verdadera, Canaán, or Betania, some of the seven churches that I pastored in Ciego de Ávila, or of the first experience in Guáimaro, Camagüey, where I replaced the Reverend Luis Villalón Rubio for a year when he was studying in Switzerland with his wife. But she was the leader who worked on whatever task was necessary without assuming a responsibility, a position, a job that did not belong to her and to which God had not called her. She has always protested when someone calls her pastor. She reacts quickly by explaining and teaching what it is like to be called by God to the pastorate. I believe that her help in my work as a pastor was better and more extensive not being a pastor, but an ideal companion in all my tasks.

No one has been more critical of me than Ormara. Given her specialty as a philologist, she has always been aware of my inappropriate expressions, my misuse of language, or the use of terms not accepted by the Language Academy. But she has not limited herself to philological criticism.

She has also been an accurate analyst of my theological and biblical interpretations. She says she knows less about these needs than I do, but her many years of Christian life have empowered her to, after listening carefully, exercise healthy and judicious criteria. Someone has said that the best friend is the most critical. That has been Ormara with me.

When I talk about our marriage, about the hard effort we have both made to become "two in one flesh," a process in which we are still immersed, I say that God blessed me with a woman superior to me but that he also rewarded me with her family. My in-laws were very close to me. I considered them and loved them as my own father and mother, especially my father-in-law, Jose M. Nolla y Domínguez, who showed me as much attention and closeness as he did with his son Waldo.

My mother-in-law, Alicia M. Cao Machado, with deep Christian convictions and a life of prayer and action, never criticized or condemned me.

On the contrary, sometimes tacitly, other times out loud, she showed me understanding and took up my defense. Waldo, Loida, and Nidia were my brothers and sisters; they still are. Special mention is deserving of the good grandmother Estefanía Machado Ruíz, that woman of God who, "without mincing words", was the most loving member of the church, but she was also the most critical towards what was done wrong.

Her youngest daughter, Lucinda, an angel of the Lord, had a gentle and sweet character but not expressive. She spent more than thirty years without participating in any activity in the church, except for our wedding. But after Estefania's departure to her place in the heavenly abode, she began to attend and actively participate in the Emmanuel Baptist Church, which I pastored. At times, she applauded me, at others, she admonished me, at all times, she loved me.

I don't think that in human experience, there have been many people as blessed as I am in relationships of love and understanding as a couple. And it is not a product of my dedication, devotion, and expressiveness, it has been Ormara.

Living According to the Circumstances

For everything narrated and for much more, she has well-earned the title of ideal help.

Living According to the Circumstances

Military Production Assistance Units (UMAP)

When writing about this stage of my life, I do so with deep gratitude to God for what it meant in my formation. I don't think there was any more enriching experience than having gone through something that, although intended to be a punishment, was turned by the Lord into the "university of life" for me.

Little has been published in the country about the Military Production Assistance Units. I only know of one article on the website of the National Center for Sexual Education (CENESEX), a department of the Ministry of Public Health, the essay "*The UMAP Generation*" by Mr. Idalberto Carbonell, the book *God Does Not Enter My Office*, written by the priest Alberto González Muñoz, and the diary of the priest Raymundo García Franco. It seems that a stage in our history wants to be buried in silence, the knowledge to which new generations do not have access.

The units were created under the Compulsory Military Service (SMO) law. Every Cuban young man who reached the age of eighteen had, by law, to register with his Municipal Military Committee and wait for his call to the ranks. However, in the opinion of those who directed these matters in the country, not all young Cubans were suitable to defend from military units the humanistic scope of the Cuban Revolution and, therefore, they considered it necessary to create specialized units for those who, they understood, were "social scourges." This is how Fidel Castro expressed it in a speech that appeared in the Granma newspaper on April 14, 1966, "The fundamental mission of the UMAP is to make these young people change their attitude, educating themselves, training themselves, saving themselves..."

"Social scourges" were people with a non-heterosexual orientation, pimps, individuals with addictions, ideologically deformed young people ("young men who did not like to work"), inmates who had served sentences and whose behavior still left much to be desired, and "the religious people." Under this last name, young pastors, seminarians, leaders of Christian denominations and churches, and practitioners of Afro-Cuban religions were called to the ranks.

We never really found out what criteria were used to select those of us who were called up. In some seminaries, there were few students; in various regions of the country, some pastors were called, while others of the same age and training were not recruited. The same thing happened in other sectors.

The Military Production Assistance Units were in the plains of the former province of Camagüey, especially in areas dedicated to the production of sugar cane. They were almost entirely isolated from the rest of the population and, in many cases, far from communication routes with nearby towns.

Living According to the Circumstances

They used to be very similar. They were built in a few months in a very discreet way. Not even their builders knew the purpose for which they were intended. They consisted of two dormitory barracks, a dining room, kitchen, offices, and hostel for the Rebel Army officers, bathrooms, and latrines. They were all surrounded by a tall chain link fence with barbed wire on top. Access was limited, and an armed soldier remained at the entrance to the unit.

In general, the soldiers in charge of the place were people with very low academic preparation and, it was said, punished for different infractions in their combat units. Many were despotic, dictatorial, and insensitive, although, as in any human conglomerate, there were exceptions.

The work regime was, at least in the first eighteen months of its creation, abusive. They woke us up at dawn, in "dead time" at 5:30 am, during the sugar cane harvest, earlier, and sometimes we worked in early morning shifts. The work was regulated and each "UMAP soldier" had to comply with the norm of the day in cutting the cane or in his cultural services. As long as we did not comply with the norm, we could not return to our shelters, not even at lunch time.

We knew little or nothing about our rights; duties were limited to daily work and "political orientation" classes, which were taught by the unit's politicians with total deficiency and ignorance of what they should share. Sometimes we were the "umapenses" themselves who read the materials since some of the "politicians" barely knew how to read.

The intention of this segregation policy was to "educate" those who, judging by the recruiters, "were deviated" in the love of the country, the defense of the Revolution, and the anti-imperialist policy. It was impossible to achieve that goal in the conditions of apparent seclusion to which we were subjected and given the incapacity of those who should be our trainers.

The first call to the UMAP was made in November 1965; I was called in the second one. I then worked as an English teacher at the Ramón Peredas Pulgares Rural Basic Secondary School, in Cascorro, province of Camagüey, of which I was also secretary and something like administrative deputy director. I did good work at school, not only from a teaching point of view but also thanks to the collaboration I provided to existing organizations.

At the time of my call, I was the organizational secretary of the Union Section. In May 1966, two months before my call-up, I had been designated National Vanguard of Secondary Education and, along with a dozen teachers of the same level from the former province of Camagüey, I received a trophy and a diploma in an activity held in the Sierra Maestra room of the Habana Libre hotel, where the Minister of Education and Army General Raúl Castro were present.

Living According to the Circumstances

However, on July 3, 1966, ten months after I was married, Dr. Salime Saker Saker, deputy provincial director of secondary education, showed up at the school to give me the summons that I had to report for Compulsory Military Service.

Ormara and I lived then on Oscar Primelles Street (San Esteban) in Camagüey. Since they still had my bachelor's address in the Military Registry, they took the summons for the ranks to my maternal home. My parents and brother were on vacation at the beach, and therefore, they could not reach me.

As the Military Committee knew of my location as a professor in Cascorro, they delivered the official summons to Dr. Saker. When she handed it to me, Dr. Saker told me, "It's about your call for compulsory military service, but we have requested that it be postponed. We need you to finish the course, there are not enough English teachers in the province." I was sure that the summons would not be for the ranks of the Military Service, so I told her, "Doctor, this is not a summons for service, this is a call to the UMAP." She used several arguments to assure me that this was not the case, and she told me that Dr. Sindulfo Sosa, director of administration of the Provincial Directorate of Education, was currently discussing the issue.

That night, Ormara and I decided to have a farewell dinner at La Volanta restaurant in front of Agramonte Park. There, we met Dr. Sosa, who told me, "Noel, don't worry about the call, you are exempt from military service." We discussed the issue deeply. "However, show up tomorrow at the place at the time indicated on the summons and they will return you to your work."

I firmly believe that Dr. Sosa made the arrangements; that was what he was informed of, but I had a feeling that it would not have any effect. That's how it was: very early in the morning of July 4, 1966, I showed up, along with approximately two hundred young people from Camagüey, at the military unit that was at the back of the then Ministry of Public Works, on the avenue that leads to the Saratoga neighborhood. There, they called about twenty people to a separate training session. Those of us who were in that group were asked, one by one, things like: What illness do you suffer from? What is your treatment? They were all people with serious and complicated illnesses.

When my turn came, and they asked me, I was forced to say, "I don't have any illness," as was true.

The officer who asked the questions then told me, "And what are you doing in this line?"

I responded, "I don't know, you called me."

From inside the barracks, a voice I did not identify said, "That's the teacher."

The officer told me, "Get on that truck immediately," and I did.

From that place, they took us to the Cándido González Stadium. I managed to call Ormara by phone, who almost immediately came accompanied by the Pentecostal pastor of the church located in the Plaza de La Habana, the Reverend Ester Quintero Labrada, who would become one of the few pastors who would spiritually attend to those of us who were in the ranks of the UMAP. It was very pleasant the time I spent there with Ormara and Ester. My wife brought me a towel, a toothbrush, toothpaste, soap, two changes of underwear, and some candy.

Around four in the afternoon, we were instructed to get back into the trucks, and we left for an unknown place. At dusk, we arrived at our destination, a place that I still cannot specify, located north of the old Jaronú power plant, today Brazil, in the Esmeralda municipality. There, they photographed those who arrived, grouped according to their characteristics, but for reasons that I still do not know, they photographed me alone.

Dusk is always nostalgic and sad for those of us who go through pressing situations. I remember that before they placed us in the barracks, which did not happen in my case, I sat on a log to ruminate on my sorrows. I felt deeply depressed. I knew nothing about my future. I could not understand how I had ended up there. I was thinking about what the education authorities had said. I was worried about how my students would finish the course, including those from the Guáimaro

Living According to the Circumstances

Basic Secondary School: their English teacher had resigned, and I was helping them prepare for the level test.

I was surprised in my musings by a young recruit who asked me permission to sit at the other end of the log. A few minutes later, he stood up in front of me and said, "Excuse me, mate, but I see you are in a bad way, don't you feel well?"

Without hiding my bad mood, I responded, "How do you think I'm going to feel good about this shit?"

Without getting upset, the young man told me, "Look, if you had confidence in the Lord and the certainty of his company, as I have, you would surely feel calmer."

I couldn't stay silent and told him, "Buddy, I've known that since I was born."

His response was very quick, "Well then, put it into practice."

The one who spoke to me was Manuel Padilla, the driver of Bishop Adolfo Rodríguez Herrera of the Catholic Diocese of Camagüey.

When I found out who it was, I was surprised: *God had sent a Roman Catholic angel to my aid!*

I believe that the experience with Padilla, with whom I shared the first two weeks of recruitment, was my conversion to ecumenism. What depth of convictions, what detachment and selflessness, what deep faith of that "Catholic angel" sent by the Lord!

Padilla and I shared a dinner of bread with bonito and a good piece of pudding that Ormara had brought me to the stadium. In the dining room, they had given something they called soup, white rice, and sardines in tomato, all in a greasy aluminum tray.

Around 10 pm, forty of us were called by names and surnames, and we got back into a truck. We didn't know what was going to happen. We simply realized that we were returning along the same path we had taken hours before.

Around midnight, we entered the city of Camagüey again. Some said with optimism and without hiding their joy, "They are returning us, they are not going to recruit us."

Hope quickly faded when we realized that the truck had taken the road to Vertientes. Late in the morning, and after passing through Vertientes and traveling along a dusty road to the south, several kilometers from the San Pedro River, they gave us instructions to get off the transport. We started walking in the middle of the darkness of a night without moon or stars for approximately one kilometer to the camp that would be our first "home" in the UMAP, Santa Susana.

I don't know how long we managed to sleep or if we slept at all. There were no beds but jute bags nailed to pieces of wood inserted into stakes. We didn't have sheets, but we did have quilts that were very useful, not to cover us but to avoid the itching caused by jute.

Still, at dawn, they got us up, and we formed lines. A long "welcome" speech was given, full of warnings and threats. At the end, we went to breakfast: coffee with something that looked like milk and a piece of bread. We had not finished when they called us back to training and gave us instructions for the work. They gave me a hoe that weighed an enormous amount, and while it was still dark, as would happen so many other times, we went to clear the cane plantations of weeds. I don't remember what my norm was, but my inability to do that type of work, the oppressive heat, the lacerating cane leaves, and the sadness weighed me down more than the hoe.

I was never able to return to the unit before two in the afternoon, I couldn't meet the norm. My luck was that working next to me was a young man from Santiago de Cuba who had played sports all his life and had a long time in his work. He was finishing his degree in Civil Engineering at the Universidad de Oriente. We talked a lot. He was the nephew of a prominent revolutionary fighter, and his uncle-in-law was a very high leader of the Revolution. They had recruited him because they considered him a "bitongo boy (a boy who didn`t like to work)." He was not at all interested in the Revolution or the heroic life of his family. He enjoyed student parties, he always walked around

Santiago with his motorcycle, and this bothered those who sent him to that "green hell." I will never forget the solidarity of that good boy. A month after being there, he told me one afternoon, when we had already arrived at the hostel, "My father traveled to Havana, he spoke with my aunt and told her what I sent him to tell him about this place. He says this is nothing like what the big bosses planned." A week later, a Rebel Army jeep arrived on a Friday evening, and my friend disappeared with those who were in it. Years later, I heard that he had taken up residence in Miami.

At home, they had no idea where they had placed me, we had no possibility of writing, much less call by telephone. Two weeks after being in Santa Susana, when I was returning from work in the furrow in a cart, I saw coming down the road a truck delivering cookies from Paloma de Castilla, the bakery that was in front of my parents' house, on Bembeta Street. I stuck my head out of the cart, trying to see who the truck driver was, and I recognized him. It was Américo Sarduy, Meco, well known to my family. I yelled at him, "Meco, tell my family that I'm in Santa Susana." They tell me that Meco went home immediately.

The following Sunday, Ormara, accompanied by my best friend, Sergio Martínez, went to try to see me. The only transport they could find on the path they took on foot from Vertientes was a car from the Cuban Petroleum Institute (ICP), a pipe car, and clinging to it, they made the journey of about fifteen kilometers to a place from where they continued walking. They arrived around eight in the morning.

Ormara had brought a good load of tasty things to eat, how much good they would have done me! But she couldn't reach the unit's fence. They held her about a hundred meters from the place. Ormara and Sergio remained waiting in the sun until about three in the afternoon for permission to see me.

At that time, one of the unit officers, whose name, thank God, I have forgotten, approached me to tell me, "Your wife is with a boy there, trying to get permission to see you. The head of the unit told me to inform her that she must leave because there are no authorized visitors. She brings you groceries, I go to pick them up and bring them to you."

Instead of being happy, I was sad thinking about how disappointing it would be for Ormara to leave without being able to see me, but I was consoled by knowing that at least she would feel happy leaving the things she brought for me. The officer returned almost immediately, and with great audacity, he told me, "Here is everything they brought you. I'm going to choose what I like and the rest, I'm going to leave it to you." My response was immediate, "Lieutenant, I don't want you to give me anything, I'm not hungry, I love eating the awful food you give." And I went to my bed, covered myself up to my head, and fell asleep crying uncontrollably. Ormara only heard the epilogue of her "bag of goodies" twenty years later.

Living According to the Circumstances

An indelible memory was left for me by two Jehovah's Witness boys who shared their fate with us in the camp. Abraham and Samuel arrived one afternoon, I don't know from what other unit. At dawn, when we were forming up to go to work, both of them refused to do so, and they were not wearing the uniform that we all wore (and I say uniform to give some name to the motley clothing with which we used to go to the sugarcane field). The two young men told the officer who was training us that they would neither wear a uniform nor work for any political regime. The more intense the boys' refusal to return to work, the more mortified the officer became. Tired of the struggle, with extreme violence, he asked them to stand in the center and shouted at them so that we could all hear clearly, "As the Bible says, who does not work does not eat, so you will remain standing here all day, and you will eat when you decide to work." We went to our tasks, and upon returning, Abraham and Samuel were still in the center of what served as the unit plaza. They hadn't eaten. When it came time to take our food, they were not allowed to do so. Many of us took the little they gave us, and when they were finally allowed to go to the barracks, we shared what we had saved for them without the guards noticing. The next day, both parties maintained the same attitude.

Many of us upon returning that afternoon, spoke with the two young Jehovah's Witnesses to try to convince them that they would lack nothing in their faith or in Jehovah by working. They did not give in to our arguments. The next day, a military transport picked them up the moment we went out into the field. We later learned that they had been arrested for "rebellion." We never heard from them again.

The first weekend of October was my first pass at the UMAP. Almost three months had passed without contact with my family. I arrived at the apartment without warning. Ormara was already ready to leave for Sunday School. I bathed faster than ever, and together, we went out. What happiness to climb the small staircase of my church in Cisneros on the corner of Hermanos Agüero in Camagüey! The first person I greeted was Brother Mario Raga, deacon of the church. What a joy! From there I called home, I announced to my parents that I was going there, that they should prepare a banquet. Not to mention the joy of both of us.

My brother was a complete, sincere, and somewhat extremist communist militant, but he frequently told me, "If I ever knew who the degenerate was who pushed you away so they could take you to the UMAP, I'll kill him." That noon at home, I saw my brother as happy as I think I had never seen him before or since.

The pass was for one week. When I returned to Santa Susana, there were instructions to move us to another camp called La Unión. There, they asked me for the unit office, and

105

from that moment on, I was freed from hard agricultural work. My time at UMAP became more bearable.

A week after being there, "umapenses" arrived from the first call that came from other camps to reinforce the harvest in those lands. Among them was Miguel Tamayo Zaldívar. He and I had studied part of our high school at the Pinson School of the Methodist Church in Camagüey. My mother and his father had worked together at the Provincial Superintendence of Schools. Tamayo was a student at the Evangelical Theology Seminary in Matanzas. He was later an Episcopal pastor and dean of the Episcopal Cathedral of Havana and bishop in Uruguay and Cuba. We keep a good friendship. Tamayo and I shared good biblical and theological discussions. At that time, it was difficult for me to understand his theological position. Mine was extremely conservative. Little by little I also had my conversion to a broader analysis of the sacred text and the interpretation of God.

One day, when we were in the shower, Tamayo caught my attention. Someone was whispering a hymn that we both knew. We went to the shower where the sound was coming from. We discovered a student from the Adventist Seminary, Ignacio Chaviano, with whom we made a great friendship. Together, we received the Sabbath on Friday afternoon and said goodbye to it on Saturday afternoon. Together, we discussed and analyzed biblical passages and doctrines. I liked to say then, and it was true, that it was encouraging to be in the middle point between an Episcopal liberal and an Adventist conservative.

Since, at that time, Ormara and I were the promoters of the work with the youth of the Baptist Convention of Eastern Cuba, I took advantage of the nights to write, together with Tamayo and Chaviano, the weekly programs for the meetings of the intermediates, which I sent to Ormara. She typed them, reproduced them on a mimeograph machine, and sent them to the churches affiliated with the convention. If some members of the Board of Directors had known that those programs were the fruit of the work of a Baptist with an Episcopalian and an Adventist, perhaps they would have burned me at the stake.

From the San Carlos 3 camp, where they had taken us at the beginning of the sugar cane harvest, they transferred me in mid-December to the unit that was behind Public Works in Camagüey. The UMAP was going through an extensive process of change. The fences had almost disappeared, the passes were more frequent and the procedures to pay for the work we did began. Until then we only received seven pesos a month. You can imagine what that meant for someone like me who earned almost three hundred.

In that unit, in Camagüey itself, I continued working in the office, which allowed me to go out every day to the Ministry of Public Works to reconcile with the employees there the work that the UMAP soldiers carried out in various construction works in the city. Every day, I could talk to my parents and Ormara. Many weekends, sometimes authorized, sometimes not, I went to my house.

One Sunday afternoon, two trucks arrived from Esmeralda. An "umapense" recruit who had arrived at the unit sat next to me in the unit park. We started talking, and I asked him, "Are you Amaryllis' husband?" to which he replied, "And are you Ormara's husband?" It was Pastor Héctor Hernández, a graduate of the Baptist Seminary of Santiago de Cuba, married to a friend of Ormara. I didn't know him, but we made a good friendship in that unit. Héctor was placed in the warehouse, so we were both in the unit all day, and that allowed us to talk a lot. Hector was then a great student of the Bible, which he read in French and English, and continued his studies of Greek in the Second Testament. I learned a lot from him.

The second quarter of 1967 brought new signs of cracking in the UMAP. The fact that the "umapenses" earned according to the norms they carried out both in agriculture and in construction, working alongside agricultural workers or in the construction sector, leaving the camps, sometimes without a guardian, and especially the fact that some groups worked in the towns near the camps or, as in the case of the city of Camagüey, in shelters located on the outskirts of the town itself, were measures that gave us clear signs of the nearness of the end.

They transferred me to a unit under construction that was at the bottom of what was then called in Camagüey El Alambique, located on the road to the airport and not far from it. Those of us who formed that company worked in construction in the city. Those who directly participated in that work left in the morning after breakfast and returned around five in the afternoon.

The facility lacked showers, and we had to bathe in a small pool of the Hatibonico river, which ran in the background or under a water tap that was about a meter high in the middle of the pasture. But no one complained about that or other inconveniences, we all remembered the confinement to which we had been subjected before.

We frequently received comments about the adverse reaction that the UMAP had and still had in the mass media abroad and about the statements of influential people from other latitudes who criticized their procedures.

It was in those days when I read the book *One Day* by *Iván Desinovich*. He was a young Baptist, like me, who had been in a labor camp in Siberia during Stalin's government. The comments that we had made so many times about the "Stalinist" measures that the UMAP had implemented paled before the ordeals that the book narrated about that "Soviet comrade in misfortune." Now, I think that the transplant of methods, concepts, and procedures was harmful to our country. Perhaps the Soviet Union helped us as a nation at crucial moments in history after 1959, but the exact imitation of that system, at least of the UMAP, left a history of bitterness, resentment, and opposition to the humanist policy of the Cuban Revolution.

In June 1967, a medical commission arrived at our unit for the first time. The ophthalmologist who was in the group examined me. It was easy for me to make my visual difficulties known: night blindness, poor visual field, and hemeralopia (difficulty adapting to light contrasts). This, together with the family history, clearly indicated a diagnosis of retinitis pigmentosa. However, the ophthalmologist did not certify my situation, with which I might obtain my discharge from the UMAP but on the contrary, she told the otorhinolaryngologist who was part of the brigade, Dr. Nelson Sosa Bada, a member of the same church as me, "That boy is pretending to get discharged. He knows the disease very well and has fabricated the information for me". Even though Dr. Sosa argued with her about my family history and the seriousness of my character, the doctor did not sign my discharge. Later I learned that she did not do it because she was sanctioned working in Camagüey for having tried to leave the country illegally. For some Havana residents there was no worse punishment than sending them to work in the plains of Camagüey or in the mountains of Oriente.

Days later, another medical commission came. On that occasion, the ophthalmologist was Dr. Mendoza, with whom I became friends years later at the Salvador Allende Hospital in Havana. After a simple examination, he made the request for my discharge for lacking the necessary conditions to continue recruiting.

A reading of the history after the almost silent disappearance of the UMAP led me to discover that many of us who had that experience became prominent leaders of the Cuban Churches: Jaime Ortega Alamino, archbishop of Havana and Roman Catholic cardinal; Miguel E. Tamayo Zaldívar, Episcopal bishop of Uruguay and Cuba; Joel Ajo Fernández, bishop of the Methodist Church of Cuba; Raúl Suárez Ramos, president of the Council of Churches of Cuba and director of the Martin Luther King Jr. Memorial Center; Raymundo García Franco, founder, and director of the Christian Center for Reflection and Dialogue; Alberto González Muños, president of the Baptist Convention of Western Cuba; Roy Acosta García, president of the Eastern Baptist Convention of Cuba; Elmer Lavastida Alfonso, founder and deputy director of the B. G. Lavastida Ecumenical Center; Samuel Entenza Reguera, rector of the Baptist Seminary of Santiago de Cuba, to name just a few. However, many others decided to take advantage of the facilities that the United States government provided and still provides to those who, having been recruits of the UMAP, request entry to that country: a resident status that protects the family unit.

Living According to the Circumstances

In November 2015, a small group of those of us who had lived the experience of the UMAP met, together with our wives, at the Christian Center for Reflection and Dialogue in the city of Cárdenas to remember the experiences lived fifty years ago. It was a magnificent moment in which Christian brotherhood and gratitude to the Lord reigned. Anecdotes, experiences, and testimonies made us laugh and cry. Gratitude to God for his always timely help prevailed, and recognition to the wives, who lived what happened inch by inch.

After more than fifty years since the first call to the UMAP, I am saddened that the Cuban Revolution, which in other matters has recognized its mistakes, has never publicly expressed the gross error that constituted those forced labor camps that were created under the protection of the Compulsory Military Service Law.

Living According to the Circumstances

The National Association Of The Blind

In the Republican era, there were some charitable entities in Cuba whose purpose was to support blind and low-vision people. All of them lacked government support and were supported by private contributions. The one that achieved the most prominence was the Varona Suárez Foundation, which bore the name of its founder. Located in Marianao, Havana, part of its work was the creation of a school for blind and low-vision people from all over the country. Varona Suárez was the only educational center for this universe of people in the entire nation.

Every month, someone would come to my house, my father would give him a sum – of which I never knew the amount – and he received a receipt for his contribution to said institution. When he became blind in 1953, Dad wrote to Varona Suárez requesting guidance to learn the reading-writing system known by the surname of its creator, Luis Braille, a young Frenchman who, after being blinded in Paris, created a magnificent method, in force to this day, which is based on six dots placed like the top of a domino. With these points, the alphabet, numbers, and punctuation marks are recreated.

Dad received the lessons from the foundation school, consisting of an aluminum sheet with the dots of the alphabet in relief and a piece of paper glued to the bottom edge with each letter printed. I helped my father in the apprenticeship process by placing the index finger of his right hand, as it was oriented, on the letter in question and telling him what it was. My father learned extremely easily and soon requested the sending of texts, which he read very quickly. Not content with what he received from Havana, he requested texts from abroad, first in Spanish and then in English.

We did not know other blind people who read Braille in Camagüey then, but we did in Havana, and my father established contact with them. He maintained a relationship, in particular, with a blind lawyer named Zacarías Albizu, who, around ten years earlier, had developed a literacy campaign for the blind through the RHC Cadena Azul radio station, which was owned by Amado Trinidad, a character noted for his defense of the most dispossessed.

Another institution that dealt to some extent with charitable care for blind people in the country was the Lions Club. In Camagüey, as in other provincial capitals, every December 13, the day of Saint Lucia, considered the patron saint of blind people, they were summoned to receive help consisting of a wooden cane painted white and red on the first twelve inches from the ground. That day, in the case of Camagüey, at the Railway Club, located in the Vigía neighborhood, they offered a lunch and, almost every year, a bag of groceries for the celebration of Christmas Eve on December 24.

Living According to the Circumstances

My father never participated in this activity that he called "the alms of the lions," but he did accept the canes from the Camagüey Lions Club, where he had a few friends. My two aunts, Luz Marina and María Rosa, and other relatives, especially Dad's cousins, did attend the lunches, but my other blind uncles, Rubén and Joaquín, did not. Carlos, also blind, but resident in Morón, never traveled for that feast.

After the revolutionary triumph of January 1, there were some attempts to create an institution for blind or visually impaired people, but it did not happen until Dr. Carlos Olivares Sánchez, the first representative of the Cuban revolutionary government in the United Nations and former Cuban ambassador in the Soviet Union, took on the task of creating an association for this universe of people in the country. He appealed to the highest levels of Cuban politics and gained the required sympathy and support. On July 19, 1975, the National Association of the Blind (ANCI) was created in Havana City.

Following the guidelines of Dr. Olivares, a management committee was organized in Ciego de Ávila to create the association at the provincial level. The Ministry of Public Health assumed coordination and put Dr. Héctor Reboredo in charge, who invited Luis Guadarrama, a blind person who worked as a physiatrist. Luis had completed his primary and secondary studies at the Varona Suárez Foundation and worked at the Antonio Luaces Iraola Provincial Hospital.

Living According to the Circumstances

My mother met Guadarrama at a cultural activity at the Teatro Principal. Seeing him walking with his white and red cane, she approached him, and they started a conversation. Later, frequent relationships continued by telephone. At the same time, Ormara needed to receive physiotherapy treatment, and Luis Guadarrama was precisely the technician who treated her. Those were the months when I was studying at Codrington College on the island of Barbados. Upon my return, Mom and Ormara told me about Guadarrama, with whom I began to relate.

When the management committee was created for the constitution of the Association of the Blind in the province, Guadarrama invited me to be part of it. Together with Dr. Héctor Reboredo, María Eugenia Cepeda, then a medical student, and others, we met on several occasions. On August 13, 1978, Fidel's birthday, the Provincial Committee of the National Association of the Blind was founded in Ciego de Ávila, an event that took place in the theater of the provincial hospital and was attended by the president of the National Association (ANCI), Dr. Carlos Olivares.

The creation of the provincial instance of the ANCI was followed by that of the Ciro Redondo municipality in November of the same year. My cousin Elio Fernández Moreda, the only one of my uncle Carlos's three children with retinitis pigmentosa, and his wife promoted the task and achieved the establishment of the ANCI in Morón, the third headquarters in the province.

Working together with Guadarrama, we achieved, with frequent visits to the remaining municipalities of the province, the creation of municipal instances. Not without effort, we obtained the premises for the operation of the Association in a house designated by the government for that purpose on Serafín Sánchez Street number 8 between Marcial Gómez and Abraham Delgado, from where we later moved to the current headquarters, located on Independence Street, today converted into the city boulevard.

In the Association, I performed two tasks in different periods: that of provincial vice president and, for several years, that of rehabilitation secretary. So, all the work of the Association at the provincial level was unpaid. We carried out the tasks in our free time, although on occasions, we obtained paid leave for the president to deal with specific issues of the organization.

Upon the death of Dr. Olivares, he was succeeded as president of the National Association by Amado González Landa, who had become blind while carrying out his duties as an officer of the Revolutionary Armed Forces. Landa never managed to shake off his military training. I had multiple working relationships with him, but they were always formal, on diplomatic occasions, but never fraternal or friendly. Landa did not understand that a Christian could be a leader of the Association. I found myself unable to participate in their first congresses. The proposal of my colleagues who proposed me in the organizational assemblies of the congresses in the province was secretly withdrawn. But thanks to the changes that have occurred since 1990 regarding believers, I participated in the sixth congress, which was held at Cuba's Communist Party (PCC) Hermanos Marañón school in Santiago de Cuba, on November 18 and 19, 2005, whose motto was "Congress, revolution, development, and integration." At the seventh congress, held at the MINSAP Convention Center in Cojímar, on November 27 and 28, 2013, the motto was "In the VII Congress, integration multiplies strength and unity." At the eighth congress, held on December 3 and 4, 2019 at the Havana Convention Palace, I attended as a guest. I was always a member of the Provincial Council of the Association, but only in 2001 I joined the National Council.

In Ciego de Ávila, we had several presidents who continued the work of Guadarrama, who, even when he no longer held the presidency of the Association, continued to give all his efforts until his death. The various presidents and their respective terms of office contributed to the growth of the organization, even though some of them caused more deterioration than development.

Living According to the Circumstances

I want to dedicate a special paragraph to the work of Eloísa Delgado Concepción. She came to the Association by the decision of the Provincial Committee of the Communist Party. In a short time, she mastered everything concerning the Organization Secretariat of the Association and she fully helped the associate who served in that role. Surprisingly, Eloísa partially lost her sense of sight as a result of macular degeneration, so from an effective collaborator, she became an associate. Chosen as organizational secretary and first vice president, she later became president of the ANCI in the province. She was a convinced materialist for whom the existence of God had no place, but she unconditionally respected my Christian opinion and never took it into account regarding our work in the Association. Out of respect for her principles, I never spoke to her about the love of God, the saving grace of Jesus Christ, or the timely help of the Holy Spirit. I am very sorry for not having done so and for having placed respect for her atheism above my duty to guide her or invite her to walk through life in the ways of Jesus Christ. But one morning, Eloísa went to the premises of the Emmanuel Baptist Church, of which I was still the pastor, and she told me, "I need to talk to you, I have something personal to let you know." I invited her to sit in my office, and she told me, "You may think I'm a crazy old woman, but I need to know about God." I did not hesitate to speak to her about the value of faith and trust in God. Without abandoning her political position and her respect for the Party's guidelines, Eloísa began to be part of our church. Her baptism was one of the happiest moments of my pastoral work. While still president of the ANCI, she shared her faith with her family. Eloísa lived her last years faithful to the Revolution, the Party, her Church, and the Lord.

I have always felt indebted to the ANCI. I think I have never given it all the effort and time it deserves. My responsibilities since 1991, first in the General Coordination of the Pastoral Care of People with Disabilities, a program of the Council of Churches of Cuba, and then in the Ecumenical Network in Defense of People with Disabilities of the World Council of Churches, in the time I served as coordinator for Latin America and member of the coordinating team prevented me from giving ANCI a greater effort.

The truth is that I have put a lot of my energy and my ability not only into blind and low-vision people in Cuba and other places in Latin America but also into all people with disabilities.

The National Association of the Blind in Cuba, and especially in Ciego de Ávila, has achieved and strives to expand the inclusion of blind and low-vision people in the work of our society, and although there is still much to do, what it has done deserves the recognition and applause to those who, with effort and tenacity, have ensured that blind and low vision people do not live on alms, but with the respect and consideration deserved from the Cuban authorities and the people in general.

Living According to the Circumstances

Ecumenism

The Christian formation of my family came from the teachings of my grandmother, América Pérez. It was transmitted to her by her father, who emigrated to Mexico after the Ten Years' War, where he became friends with José Martí, who gave him the Bible that my grandmother kept throughout her life. When my great-grandfather returned during the Fruitful Truce, he understood the faith very differently from the Roman Catholic tradition in which he had been raised.

The religious culture in which my grandmother was raised under the protection of her father, who died when she was very young, turned her into an enemy of Catholicism. She was one of the first people baptized in the city of Camagüey when the Reverend David A. Wilson began the work of what was the First Baptist Church of that city. She considered herself, above all, a Baptist. For my grandmother, even passing through the door of a Catholic temple was wrong; that was the "kingdom of idolatry."

When my parents decided to enroll me in the Pinson School of the Methodist Church because there was no Baptist work-teaching institution in Camagüey, she did not see it favorably and argued that there were many better schools than that one. I felt very fulfilled at Pinson, but students from Baptist families argued with the Methodists and tried to be better in every way, something like the truly saved.

Living According to the Circumstances

My brother's decision in his early youth to leave the congregation of First Baptist Church of the city for being "very cold" and joining the Evangelical Pentecostal Church, Assemblies of God, "because they live the fire of the Spirit," almost made my grandmother, who called Pentecostals scandalous extremists, collapse.

Despite those far from ecumenical feelings, she was a source of inspiration for many people, especially for me. My grandmother's Christian experience and solid faith, her conservative and anti-ecumenical theology, bore fruit worth remembering. Her devotion and testimony reflected the sincere and total dedication of a human being to the teachings of Jesus Christ.

My church had certain contradictions. Although it participated in the monthly services that were held with other non-Catholic congregations in the city - Episcopalians, Methodists, Nazarenes, and Pentecostals - it made strong criticisms of the Council of Evangelical Churches of Cuba, of which it had been a founding member of the Baptist Convention of Eastern Cuba, to which our church was affiliated. When the Christian Student Movement (MEC) became strong, and one of the theological modules that did so much good for my generation arrived in Camagüey, the pastor had them in his office and surely read them. However, our congregation looked askance at the MEC and its leaders. Ormara was the founder of that ecumenical movement at the Central University of Las Villas, when she was studying Philosophy and Letters in the first half of the 1960s. However, I refused to participate in the movement and, along with other young people in my congregation, criticized it.

My conversion to ecumenism was one of the positive results of my call to the UMAP. I owe it to the support of an "angel of the Lord" of Catholic origin and to close relations with an "episcopal liberal" and an "Adventist conservative."

My first responsibility in the ecumenical world came as a result of my participation in the Youth Department of the Council of Evangelical Churches of Cuba. Then president and priest Héctor Méndez Rodríguez invited me to join that area of work of the Council together with the Reverend Elmer Lavastida (Eastern Baptist), Dimas Hidalgo (Methodist), Emilio Martín (Episcopal), Adolfo Pandiello (Free Baptist) and Orestes González Jr. (Presbyterian). I thank Héctor Méndez for his trust in me and also for later accepting me as one of the leaders in Cuba of the Latin American Union of Ecumenical Youth (ULAJE). By virtue of this, I had the privilege of accompanying him to two events: first to the Continental Assembly in Ñaña, Peru, in 1976, and to Panama in 1980 to participate in the meeting Human Rights, Rights of the People. Later I joined the Laity Commission of the Council of Churches, from where I was able to continue participating fully in the work of Cuban ecumenism.

When I moved to Ciego de Ávila in September 1968, I found a church more open to ecumenical thought than the one in the city of Camagüey, where I had grown up. The Reverend Marino Santos Martínez, who had pastored that congregation for ten years (1955-1965), had been, along with Santiago Entenza and Álida Barrios, one of the few Eastern Cuban Baptists who had completed theological studies at the Evangelical Seminary of Theology in Matanzas before the 1960s, in addition to having been a prominent young man in the Independent Baptist Convention. The Independent Baptists, who were a detachment from the Eastern Convention, had no relations of any kind with the latter and even less with its Bible Institute, located in the International Colleges of El Cristo. It was for this reason that Marino studied in Matanzas. Upon completing his studies, instead of returning to his roots, he accepted a job offer with the Eastern Convention and went to pastor in Ciego de Ávila. His ecumenical thinking, acquired in the relationship with Methodists, Presbyterians, Episcopalians, and Quakers in Matanzas, determined the orientation of the First Baptist Church of Ciego de Ávila. There, I found notebooks for the various Sunday School classes written by the Presbyterian Church, as well as the notebooks for the Spanish American Course, written by Baptist educators from Eastern Cuba together with

Methodists, Presbyterians, and Episcopalians from Cuba and the rest of Latin America. I worked with these materials at various times as a Sunday School teacher.

Gilberto Prieto Socarrás replaced Reverend Marino Santos in the pastorate of the First Baptist Church in Ciego de Ávila, and although he lacked ecumenical training like Marino's, he never expressed himself against ecumenical relations between the various aspects of Cuban Christianity. In Ciego de Ávila, relations with Catholics, Adventists, Pentecostals, and Episcopalians, the best known of the few denominations based in the city in those years, were common in the First Church and especially in Gilberto Prieto. In the only Catholic church in the city, there were two priests who established fraternal and affectionate relationships with Ormara and me, and with the church. This approach was promoted by María Antonia Armengol Gómez, Maruja, a very close friend of Ormara, leader of that church who shared with us not only an unbreakable friendship but also fidelity to the Lord through her Roman Catholic tradition. With Maruja, we attended various events and acquired friendships that have lasted to the present.

One of those priests, Adolfo Guerra, was a true example of loyalty to the Lord, modesty, and Christian brotherhood. We admired him for his dedication to the cause of Jesus Christ and for his camaraderie. The other, Félix Padrón, even asked his bishop for permission to attend our wedding, which was not allowed because it was not a sacramental act. However, work reasons prevented him from being present at our wedding, which took place on a Sunday at seven in the morning, the time when he had to officiate at a mass.

A true ecumenical consciousness was the one that developed from the work carried out by the Baptist Student Workers Coordination of Cuba (COEBAC). Although this movement fundamentally brings together Baptists, its postulates, its scope, and its actions were and continue to be remarkably ecumenical. It was not easy to get COEBAC granted membership in the Council of Churches. This request and this manifest interest on the part of the organization were opposed by some leaders of Cuban Presbyterianism, who, apparently, felt challenged by the young and vigorous leadership that we represented at that time. Fortunately, not everyone in that denomination, or in others, had that criterion. The acceptance of COEBAC as a full member of the Council was for us, more than a possibility of ecumenical action, a challenge.

The practical ecumenism developed in the olden province of Camagüey deserves a separate paragraph. Significant were the affection and solidarity of the Reverend Ester Quintero Labrada, pastor of the city's Evangelical Pentecostal Church, perhaps the largest of that denomination on the island. During her pastorate, Ester worked for the unity of the city's Christians: Methodists,

Episcopalians, Nazarenes, and Baptists were accompanied at various times by this sister, and she, in turn, received the support and solidarity of the other congregations. Our pastor, the Reverend Rafael Gregorich, collaborated with the Pentecostal church. In it, he preached, officiated at wedding ceremonies, and gave communion.

These relationships had their genesis on September 24, 1938, when services began in Camagüey under the auspices of the Assemblies of God. A missionary from Puerto Rico, Belén Nieves, who was the mother of a son with intellectual disabilities, received support from the almost newly minted pastor of the city's First Baptist Church, Reverend Gregorich. Young troubadours from the congregation helped the missionary in her worship. Later, in 1950, an American missionary, T. L. Osborn, visited that nascent Pentecostal congregation and evangelism and divine healing services were held at the Guarina ball stadium, to which Pastor Gregorich and the congregation he pastored also gave their support, as well as the Methodist pastor Reverend Víctor L. Rankin, Dr. Moisés Boudet, director of the Pinson College, and the Reverend Agustín González, of the Episcopal Church. As a result of that campaign, some families came to the feet of the Lord and to the membership of our church in Camagüey, among which that of Luis Guerra and Esperanza Pérez stood out. They were the parents of Nancy and María Guerra. Nancy was the first leader of that church and a faithful collaborator of the Pastoral Care of People with Disabilities, the program of the Council of Churches of Cuba that I coordinated for almost thirty years. For twenty-five of them, Nancy was part of its coordinating team.

The fraternity and fellowship among Camagüeyan Christians in the 1950s and 1960s gradually became a concrete ecumenism that even involved some young Catholic priests. At the beginning of the 1970s, from the town of Céspedes first and then from Guáimaro, a young Baptist pastor, Luis Villalón Rubio, who had written his thesis on ecumenism after graduating with a bachelor's degree in Theology at the Baptist Seminary of Santiago de Cuba, brought together young pastors and priests for analysis and reflection in a very positive intellectual effort. For his part, the Reverend Juan Ramón de la Paz Cerezo, rector of the San Pablo Episcopal Church in Camagüey, joined forces in a practical ecumenism that, together with the intellectual efforts promoted by the Reverend Villalón, achieved a cohesion never seen at that territory and perhaps in others in the country.

Based on the impulse and organization of Juan Ramón de la Paz, Luis Villalón, Eduardo Pedraza, and Ester Quintero, among others, Christian leaders carried out the first productive and socially useful work in agricultural and other facilities. That little-known and much less recognized movement was the embryo of what would later become common in some sectors of the Cuban Church.

Ormara greatly surpassed me in ecumenical work. Formed by her pastor, Marino Santos, and a church more open than mine, during her studies at the Central University of Las Villas, she had resided in the Presbyterian Home, a job supported by the Church of that denomination in Santa Clara under the pastorate of the presbyter Carlos Camps Cruell. This facility provided paid accommodation and food to young students from provinces and towns near the University. That experience contributed to Ormara standing out for integral ecumenism. Founder of the Christian Student Movement in Santa Clara, later involved in the Council of Churches, she coordinated two of its departments: Church Renewal (between 1993 and 1995) and Women (from 1995 to 2000). She also held the vice presidency of the Council on two occasions: between 1989 and 1993 and from 2000 to 2002. In that last period, she was the first vice president and was replaced at various times by Dr. Reinerio Arce Valentín, who was then president of the Council.

Ormara's contribution to Cuban ecumenism has also been relevant through the World Day of Prayer (WDP), of which she was regional coordinator for Central America, the Hispanic Caribbean, and greater Colombia (from 2003 to 2012), and later coordinator of its national team from 2011 to 2017. In this performance, her most relevant performance was the preparation and development, together with the WDP National Committee and other women leaders, of the World Day of Prayer in 2016, when Christian women in all parts of the world prayed for Cuba motivated by the program prepared in our country and distributed worldwide by that movement.

My participation in ecumenism crossed national borders. I first became involved in events in Latin America through my work in the Latin American Union of Ecumenical Youth (ULAJE). Thanks to a recommendation from Dr. Ofelia M. Ortega, I participated in Geneva, Switzerland (1994), in a meeting about the need to include the issue of disability in the agendas of the Churches under the auspices of the World Council of Churches. It was the opening to an ecumenical task on a global scale that brought me many blessings and the acquisition of knowledge that otherwise would not have been within my reach.

A phrase that my mother-in-law used to repeat – "You have to love people as they are and not as you want them to be" – contributed a lot to making me understand the point of view of others, not only in relation to faith but also to politics. The ecumenism that I have practiced after my conversion to it has been more than part of a Christian formation, a way to understand God's project of life and hope in Jesus Christ.

During my pastorate in Emmanuel, the doors of our facilities were always open to all faiths and all actions that served to dignify human beings. With joy and love, we serve local churches, but above all we promote meetings and activities not always accepted by other congregations but blessed by the Lord. Ciego de Ávila is not a place with a mentality open to diversity. The experience we brought from Camagüey was very different, but we made an effort and achieved something.

The ecumenical nature of the Pastoral Program for People with Disabilities of the Council of Churches of Cuba, which I have coordinated since 1991, deserves special mention. In all the Pastoral actions, Christians from all officially registered confessions in our country have participated in full harmony. The national Pastoral team that has organized the program efforts has always been made up of people of various faiths. Sister Dinorah Ayala Sierra also deserves special mention. She was a member of the religious order of the congregation of the Missionary Sisters of the Immaculate Conception (MIC) for twenty-two years, and after leaving the cloister, was part of our work as coordinator of the subprogram of attention to collaborators. Dinorah has been a faithful assistant and invaluable encourager and advisor in my work, and she has taught me many things about her Roman Catholic religious tradition that have been very useful to me in my ecumenical work.

Without a doubt, ecumenism in Cuba, in the dimension that I understand to be correct, was born when the Council of Evangelical Churches of Cuba was created on May 31, 1941. In my opinion, the transformative renaissance that was taking place in the country with the approval of the 1940 Constitution determined the birth of a project that had been cherished for many years before an institutional movement that would bring together Protestant Christians in the country. The initial motto of the Council, which is still the motto of the Council of Churches of Cuba – "United to Serve" – is demonstrative of the objectives set.

The Council dealt with an almost non-existent social work demanded by a mediatized republic seasoned by corruption, plunder, and perks. The Churches became involved in the first literacy campaign waged on the island with a German teaching method. The temples became schools, and the pastors became teachers. Jointly, a program was developed to eradicate prostitution, drugs, vices, and corruption. Also, in the unity of the evangelical people, the perks that the governments in power granted to the Catholic Church were censored, which, by receiving government aid, managed to establish schools, dispensaries, orphanages, homes for the elderly, etc.

As I have already mentioned, my congregation, the First Baptist Church in Camagüey, did not claim to be ecumenical, but my pastor, the Reverend Rafael Gregorich Escalona, adopted positions that, in my opinion, defined him as such.

The departure of the Baptist Convention of Eastern Cuba from membership of the Council in 1964 was, in my opinion, due to the political confrontation, which was experiencing a crescendo in the evangelical and/or Protestant congregations of the country. The Council, with its broad vocation for service, made frequent declarations of solidarity with social objectives of national and international impact. Some leaders of member denominations, such as those of the Eastern Convention, disagreed, preferring, they said, to take an "apolitical" position.

After the departure of the Eastern Baptist Convention, the Los Pinos Nuevos Evangelical Association and the Episcopal Church of Cuba – which later returned to the Council – followed in their footsteps. Perhaps at some moments there were biased actions and positions of the Council that transcended what was correct, but, in general, the intentions were honest and necessary.

As I already said, my conversion to ecumenism occurred during my time in the UMAP. This process deepened as the years passed, and I understood the value of unity in the midst of diversity and the need for a testimony in which the acceptance of the point of view and the interpretation of the other were valued instead of denigrating them.

Living According to the Circumstances

Methodism

In the 1950s – perhaps even earlier – and until the mid-1960s, Camagüey was an interdenominational, perhaps even ecumenical, plaza. Then, there were only eight evangelical and/or Protestant denominations: Methodists, Nazarenes, Pentecostal Evangelicals, Adventists, Episcopalians, Gideons, Baptists, and Pentecostal Christians. However, Camagüey was not an easy place for the establishment of evangelical and/or Protestant churches.

At that time, there were between twenty and thirty places in the city where masses were celebrated. Of these, eighteen were temples, the others were chapels in the many Catholic schools, nursing homes, and convents.

Protestantism was established in the early 20th century with the establishment of the First Baptist Church, founded by the Reverend David A. Wilson. That denomination managed to build two other temples in the 1950s, located in the Nadales and Garrido districts.

The other significant evangelical group was the Pentecostal movement, which gained momentum in 1952 when the American Evangelist T. L. Osborne organized a campaign of evangelism and divine healing in the facilities of the Guarina baseball stadium in what is now the El Retiro neighborhood in front of the current bus terminal. It is extremely interesting that the established churches collaborated with the Pentecostals, and instead of losing membership, they gained new followers due to the enthusiasm and knowledge of the Bible that the campaign cemented. One of the people who became markedly close to the growing Pentecostal movement was the wife of Panchito Arredondo, who shortly after became the mayor of the city. Through this lady, the Evangelical Pentecostal Church, then with a temple at the end of Maximiliano Ramos Street, obtained land owned by the city council in what was then called Plaza de La Habana, where the Hallelujah temple was built, the largest of its time of that denomination.

However, the best-known Protestants, although less numerous than the Baptists and Pentecostals, were the Methodists. They had their temple on the corner of Avellaneda and San Martín, but at the beginning of the 1950s, they sold it and built two new buildings for public worship. One was located on the corner of Julio Sanguily and Joaquín de Agüero, in the La Vigía neighborhood, with the name of San Marcos Methodist Church. The other was on the corner of Estrada Palma – today Ignacio Agramonte – and Camagüey avenues, on the grounds of Colegio Pinson, property of that denomination, with the name of San Pablo Methodist Church (today Tabernacle of the Anointing). They also had three other public preaching places: the mission on Cielo Street on the corner of Mata Street, another mission in the Garrido neighborhood, and the third in the Buena Vista neighborhood.

Pinson School was one of the best in the city. Since there was no Baptist school in Camagüey, my brother and I studied there for a few years. I felt very close to Methodism. I liked the order of their worship, the interior beauty of their temples, the peacefulness of their liturgies, and the good taste of their public celebrations. I admired the Reverend Victor L. Rankin, pastor of San Pablo, and the Reverend Cortizo, pastor of San Marcos. Reverend Rankin was a public figure who participated in both the Rotary Club and the Lions Club, but he was also an important character in the services that took place every first Monday of the month in different temples with the presence of members of all the denominations of the city, except for the Adventists and the Gideons.

Since my student days at Pinson, I not only learned about the genesis of Methodism and its doctrinal emphases, but also its national leaders. However, I was not convinced by infant baptism or the episcopal government.

While still living in Camagüey and later residing in Ciego de Ávila, we carried out several ecumenical activities in San Pablo and also in the Wesley building of the Methodists. The pastorate in San Pablo of the Reverend Pedro Mayor in the early part of the 1960s and the charisma of his wife, Ana Luisa Puertas, won our sympathy. Ormara, who at the time was the director of the choir of the First Baptist Church of Camagüey, added it to the one existing in San Pablo to perform an unforgettable Christmas concert that was presented in both churches with an unusual attendance for the time. The Reverend Mayor, a pastor by vocation and dedication, frequently visited my house to pray with my parents when we had already established our residence in Ciego de Ávila. Given the pastoral neglect to which they were subjected by the Baptist pastor on duty, the Mayor's attention earned him the affection and gratitude of my father and my mother.

In Ciego de Ávila, they did not have a Methodist congregation. It had existed and even had its temple. I do not know – nor do I believe that Methodist historians have been able to find out – why that congregation disappeared in the second half of the 1930s, although its wooden temple remained standing until July 1980 on the corner of Independence and 6th Street, in the Vista Alegre neighborhood. It was a butcher shop, a vegetable sales stand, and a branch of the Committee for the Defense of the Revolution.

However, the Methodists had three congregations in the province: Violeta (Primero de Enero), Pina (Ciro Redondo), and Morón. They were strong congregations with magnificent buildings, and all three had schools owned by the Church. In two of them, Violeta and Pina, there was no other established evangelical group, and in the case of Morón, where there were

Baptist, Episcopal, and Adventist congregations, the Methodists were the best known, and those who had the most attendees in their activities.

The triumph of the Revolution and the declaration of its socialist character weakened Methodism in the country and, of course, also in the province. Three people remained in Violeta committed to the church. One of them, Hilda Torres, told us that she opened the temple on Tuesdays and Sundays, and she prayed, read the Bible, and even sang alone... just in case the other two sisters arrived. The same fate befell the temple in Pina, larger than that of Violeta. Her "survivors" were five women who were older and had less leadership capacity than Violeta's. In Morón, the presence was greater, but also, as in the other two places, they lacked leaders and, for months, pastors.

In 1987, a young man with no Christian background, no pastoral experience, and little biblical knowledge arrived at the Methodist pastorate in Pina. He was an applicant for the seminary and had to prove his vocation in that work. The Reverend Joel Ajo, then pastor of the Methodist Church of El Vedado, a friend of ours and fellow fighter in the Cuban ecumenical movement, especially in the MEC, recommended that he locate us, and he did so. We became collaborators with young Ricardo Felipe. We frequently went to Pina so that Ormara could help by playing the out-of-tune piano there. We received him at home very frequently, we organized ecumenical activities in Pina and welcomed him as another spiritual son of ours.

At Ricardo's suggestion, we also began to help with music in the other two Methodist churches, all with pianos that were out of tune and abandoned due to lack of pianists. Loida, Ormara's sister, and her two daughters, still children but with a musical vocation, joined this effort. From these periodic cooperative visits arose the creation of a choral group that rehearsed in Morón on Sunday afternoons and sang on special occasions in some of those churches. One year they even participated in the Annual Conference held in the Methodist Church of El Vedado, in Havana City. We did not have our own transportation, so the train was an ideal means of getting there, braving the cold or the rain. It was a very beautiful experience because it brought us closer to congregations that opened their hearts to those who helped them. Furthermore, it allowed us to use our gifts, rejected by the First Baptist Church of Ciego de Ávila, which had expelled us.

At the beginning of 1988, the bishop of the Methodist Church, Armando Rodríguez Borges, decided to exchange a house owned by the church in Santiago de las Vegas for one in Ciego de Ávila. The aim was for the property to become a place for the pastors and leaders of the denomination, who traveled from one end of the island to the other, with a place to rest and regain strength. At the initiative of the young pastor Felipe, we planned to use this property to hold Methodist services in the city. Although, given the situation at the time, it seemed like a crazy project, we went together to the Registry of Associations to request permission to hold worship services there. Once the request was made, we waited three months for the response, which was affirmative, with some recommendations: give the Registry a schedule of public activities, not have celebrations that would disturb the neighbors, not overflow with attendees the limits of the room intended for worship, and to maintain a Registry of Associations of unfavorable situations that could arise with the neighborhood. The activities began with a Sunday School every Sunday morning that we attended with the family, Hilda Torres, who had recently moved from Violeta to the city of Ciego de Ávila, and one or another person that we managed to invite. The Methodist church of El Vedado donated six benches. With our offerings, we bought a piano and managed to return Methodism to the city of Ciego de Ávila.

We left there under the pastorate of Margarita Obregón, a pastor well-grounded in the Methodist tradition, when very different positions were already emerging, extremely conservative and incapable of a renewal of any nature. My in-laws chose to isolate themselves from the congregation when the pastor decided to baptize an infant, we did it later due to the inflexibility of that good woman.

Living According to the Circumstances

Although some leaders of Methodism, friends of ours, tried to convince us to join that denomination and even gave us participation in national events of the same, including annual conferences, there was never in our minds and hearts the desire to stop being part of our Baptist tradition, which despite errors and disagreements we had assumed as part of our own existence.

The withdrawal of the Methodist Church from the Evangelical Seminary of Theology in Matanzas, of which it had been a founder in 1946 together with the Episcopal and Presbyterian Churches, marked a strong break with ecumenism in that denomination. The process of withdrawal of Methodism from the Seminary left a bitter taste among Cuban Christians knowledgeable about the history of Cuban Protestantism.

In a meeting, the Methodist bishop, Ricardo Pereira, told the members of the central structure of the denomination that he did not want any Methodist to participate in activities organized by the Presbyterians and much less that they attended their temples and institutions. A month after these misguided instructions, Pastor Pedro Mayor died in the city of Santa Clara. Among his many pastorates he had served in that city, where he was in the care of his daughter, Ana Mayor Puerta. This woman, when her father died, took the necessary steps to hold his funeral at the city's funeral home, which she could not achieve because there was no capacity in that public facility at that time.

Living According to the Circumstances

The fact of living in a small apartment in the city also prevented her from watching over her father's body in her house.

Without hesitation, she went to meet the Methodist pastor to ask him for visitation and the service in the temple or the parsonage, which, in her opinion, would be the ideal place. The pastor flatly refused, which greatly harmed the already distraught sister. Someone suggested that she ask for the temple of the Presbyterian church in the city, and the pastor of the same, without thinking and without any hesitation, opened the doors of the temple that Saturday night and all Sunday until the funeral.

I had the privilege of being appointed by the Council of Churches of Cuba to deliver the sermon of thanksgiving for the life of the Reverend Mayor, given the impossibility of other directors traveling to Santa Clara. Upon arriving, I met Bishop Pereira, who arrived at the same time. He also spoke a few words about the life of that champion of the Cuban Church. He was one of the few Methodist pastors who did not leave the country in the stampede that occurred after the declaration of the socialist character of the Revolution on April 16, 1961, and the subsequent nationalization of education in Cuba, which caused the loss of the many school institutions that Methodism had throughout the national territory.

Over the years, the small Methodist congregation in the city of Ciego de Ávila grew. Our relationship with it, less frequent, continued until the departure of Reverend Alfredo González Caraballosa to occupy the pastorate of the Central Methodist Church of Havana. His successor never gave us the fraternity to which we were accustomed in relations with that denomination. The house that we had managed to convert into a temple at the end of the 1980s was exchanged for one in very poor construction condition but located in a more convenient location and with more land. There, the construction of a beautiful and modern temple began, which was dedicated to the Lord on February 8, 2019.

A few months before, we had visited the Methodist pastor to invite him to a meeting of all the evangelical and/or Protestant churches of Ciego de Ávila on the topic of disability, which would take place in the facilities of the First Baptist Church. He did not attend or send anyone despite having said he would. On that visit, I told him the history of Methodism in the city of Ciego de Ávila, and he announced to me that he would send a person to my house to take that data. We never received that visit.

The dedication of the new temple to the Lord was an event of overflowing joy for the Methodists. Attendance exceeded the place of worship, but, unfortunately, the remaining Christian communities in the city were not invited.

Living According to the Circumstances

The Baptist Student Worker Coordination Of Cuba

It is no secret to anyone that the Churches in Cuba were not prepared for the political change that the revolutionary irruption of January 1959 brought us. Although the early times were characterized by popular euphoria and revolutionary effervescence, this was no longer a reality in the majority of Christian congregations in the country.

In the Baptist churches affiliated with the Eastern Convention, a broad feeling of rebellion had arisen during the years of revolutionary struggle. Many young people from various congregations had performances worthy of relevance in the work to overthrow the Batista dictatorship that caused so much pain and anguish to the Cuban people. Lives like those of Josué and Frank País, Oscar Lucero, the Díaz brothers, Fabio Rosell, and many others awakened a greater patriotic commitment in the youth of my time.

It is worth remembering that in all the Baptist churches in the provinces of Camagüey and Oriente, national dates were commemorated with what used to be called patriotic evenings, in which with songs and poems, the patriotism of our heroes and the libertarian struggle of which as Christians we lived with pride were exalted.

Living According to the Circumstances

In that feeling of patriotism and revolutionary change, we grew and developed. The Eastern Baptist churches were creators of conscience and feelings of deep and true Cuban idiosyncrasy. Those feelings were born with the religious denomination itself. The first national pastors and missionaries had been, almost entirely, fighters for Cuban independence before and during the War of Independence. Unfortunately, many of these pastors and leaders were replaced by American missionaries who were sent to our country by the United States Domestic Mission Board after the first Yankee intervention in Cuban affairs (1898-1902).

The members of our grandparents' generation – Estefanía Machado, Ormara`s grandmother, and América Pérez, my grandmother, in Ciego de Ávila and Camagüey, respectively – had been Baptist leaders in the first years of the constitution of the respective churches and they remembered those Mambises pastors: Pedro Deulofeu, José Regino O'Halloran, Pablo Valdés and others. From them, we learned about their missionary zeal, their patriotic fervor, and their feeling of rejection of impositions in all orders that came from the "unruly and brutal North that despises us."

However, the lack of biblical and theological support for a revolutionary change of magnitude that occurred on Cuban soil after 1959 determined that my generation was divided into three large groups.

Living According to the Circumstances

1) those who emigrated to the United States "because it was impossible to live one's faith in Jesus Christ in a communist society."

2) those who abandoned their Christian commitment and their fidelity to the Church "because they wanted to carry out studies that would not be allowed in the new society if they continued living their Christian faith."

3) those who, through thick and thin, decided to stay in the Church. This last group, the smallest of the three, very soon fragmented into two: those who wanted to turn the Church into a ghetto, a refuge to isolate themselves from the world, and those of us who wanted to bear witness to our faith in a changing society, that is, a living faith in the Lord participating in the construction of his Kingdom everywhere without letting ourselves be carried away by the dichotomy between the religious and the profane, the Christian and the worldly, the spiritual and the material, the evangelical and the Marxist.

This group was not well regarded by their congregations, much less by the Baptist hierarchy of the three conventions based in the country. Deeply painful was that it was not well received in society in general, as Ormara would express on April 2, 1990, to the Cuban president, Fidel Castro, in the famous interview of seventy-six Cuban evangelical and Protestant leaders, which lasted for nine and a half hours and was televised in its entirety throughout the country.

Although the work and student misunderstandings towards Christians who tried to be an integral part of the process of change without abandoning the Christian commitment and fidelity to our Churches was very painful to us, we felt more the marginalization of which little by little we were being subjected in our local churches and denominational structures.

A group of Baptist pastors attended an activity held in 1970 at the Evangelical Theology Seminary in Matanzas. They began conversations to unite efforts and wills among those of us who, from the Church, wanted to give an effective testimony of the faith in today's Cuba. That group, which included Francisco Rodés, Luís Villalón, Orlando González, Joel Rosales, Livio Díaz, and others, agreed to begin its efforts with the periodic production of an informative organ that would contribute to the formation and training of young Baptists of the whole country. The two issues of the publication, which bore the name *El Bautista Informado*, were printed on a mimeograph machine. Its editors were, for the eastern part, the Reverend Joel Rosales, and for the western part, the pastor Francisco Rodés. That group was enriched with the incorporation of lay people, among whom were included Ormara and I, a few months after the initial agreements began to be finalized.

In June 1970, I was invited to present a topic at the Baptist Youth Convention that was held in Camagüey. My presentation caused a lot of disgust to some who looked contemptuously at those of us who, without denying our faith, maintained a testimony of commitment to the aspirations of well-being and progress of our people. The discussion that my presentation sparked that afternoon, in which some young people and leaders of the Convention participated, defined our position within the Eastern Convention.

A year later, a fellowship of young Baptists from the two conventions was held at the El Calvario Baptist Church in Havana: the Eastern and the Western convention. They had asked me to present the topic "The existence of a new morality." If before in Camagüey, my statements had provoked great diatribes and frontal opposition, those now were of greater magnitude. The wife of the pastor of a church affiliated with the Western Convention said: "Ignore him, he ends up joining the Party and abandoning the faith." (She did not abandon the faith, but she assumed political positions of commitment to the Revolution several years later). From then on, we were never invited to present topics, preach, or assume responsibilities in the Eastern Convention, we even suffered rejection and marginalization when visiting churches in which we had previously been received with the fraternity and affection that is part of the Christian vocation.

The agreements of the Baptist World Alliance at its Tokyo assembly in the late 1970s, the struggle for civil rights of black Christians in the United States under the leadership of the

Reverend Martin Luther King Jr., and other forward positions of Baptist leaders in various latitudes fueled the aspirations of the group of pastors and lay people which was centered around *El Correo Bautista*, a publication to which *El Bautista Informado* had given way.

Number five of that magazine was already circulating when Luis Villalón, Dinorah Mata, Francisco Rodés, Lilian Gonzalez, José Ferrer, Ormara, and I met to organize what would be the First National Camp on Christian Social Responsibility. This activity, which took place at the National Camp of the Presbyterian Church (CANIP), located at kilometer 11 of the highway to Camajuaní, in May 1973, brought together more than twenty-five young people, pastors, and lay people from churches affiliated with the Eastern and Western conventions. Together we analyzed biblically and theologically the historical moment in which we lived and the necessary action of the Church to give a real testimony of our faith. The final declaration of that activity has not yet lost its validity.

We, young Cuban Baptists, concerned about the challenge that the historical moment that our society was experiencing presents to the Christian faith met to analyze the most consistent projection of our action in the light of the Holy Scriptures.

Living According to the Circumstances

Inspired by the desire that other young people with these same concerns be informed of what have been the fruits of our reflections, we presented the following:

About our work

a) Analyzing the history of our work, we realized the fact that it has never been outside political issues since there has always been a defined participation of pastors and laypeople in the different political situations that our country has experienced. This spirit of participation was reflected in the celebration of patriotic events in churches, as well as in the participation of some in the electoral life and then others in the insurrectional fight against tyranny. The freedom of political options in the work was always respected.

b) Considering the above, in light of Baptist principles, we did not see any contradiction with the principle of separation of Church and State since this does not oppose the responsibility of the Christian as a citizen. Suffice it to remember that a previous president of the Baptist World Alliance carried out the presidency of the Alliance simultaneously with that of his own nation. Therefore, we were surprised that those of us who had opted for an open option of supporting the Revolution were accused of violating Baptist principles, and we wondered if there was sincerity in wielding a Baptist principle only against those of us who supported the Revolution.

c) Where a violation of the Baptist principle of freedom of conscience is observed is in the evident and repeated perceptions that lay people and pastors who assume an attitude of renewal are subject to.

d) We noted with pain the painful result of deficient training of our youth for full and responsible participation in social duties, which brought with it a dangerous dichotomy between their religious life and their social activity. We considered it the duty of the churches to help the Christian "so that he may be thoroughly prepared for a good work" (2 Timothy 3:17).

Our revolution

a) When analyzing the implications of Christian responsibility at the current moment, we realized that it is inadmissible to try to maintain thought and action outside the revolutionary situation that our country was experiencing. We believed that the alleged neutrality advocated by many hides a reactionary position.

b) On the other hand, there was a dangerous opportunistic tendency on the part of those who conditioned their participation to the benefits that may arise for the Church. We believed that the primary interest of the Church is humanity, and it must sympathize and support everything that contributes to full human fulfillment.

c) In our concrete experience, the Christian finds a favorable framework for his social responsibility in the revolutionary process of our country.

d) We considered it Christian to recognize that our revolution has taken concrete and irreversible steps in favor of humanity and that the construction of a socialist society offers the conditions for the flourishing of the Christian values of human generosity and solidarity.

Our commitment

a) We rejected the fact that, under multiple pretexts, young people committed to the revolutionary situation were marginalized.

b) At the same time, we considered inconsequential those young people who, shielded by progressive positions, avoided giving their contribution to the life of the Church.

c) We recognized the duty to give our renewing contribution to the Church in Cuba through the current structures and/or outside them.

d) We rejected the position of those who evade their social commitments by pretexting a false concept of spirituality, forgetting the example of our Lord, who approached all persons free of prejudices and fears. We believe that there is no biblical basis that prevents us from revolutionary commitment but, on the contrary, inspires us to greater dedication in favor of humanity.

e) We declared our unwavering hopes for the future of our country and in believers of good faith who know how to respond to the challenge of the present hour.

We left CANIP ready to carry out the project of articulating a movement capable of bringing together those of us with a thought as radical as the Gospel itself, who united our practice of faith with revolutionary commitment.

In November of the following year, during the celebration of the Theological Day of the East, which was held annually under the auspices of the Study Center of the Council of Churches and which on that occasion was held in the Los Amigos church in Holguín, a group composed of Livio Díaz, Raquel Cardona, Elmer Lavastida, Gisela Pérez, Juan Tejeda, Luis Villalón, Ruth Troyano and I got together to constitute a movement capable of bringing together Baptists from the three conventions eager to work for "an effective testimony in today's Cuba and the contemporary world." This movement was given the name of the Baptist Student Workers Coordination of Cuba (COEBAC). The Reverend Livio Diaz Rodríguez, at the time pastor of the Second Baptist Church of Santiago de Cuba, was elected general secretary, and I was elected organizational secretary.

COEBAC would promote the participation of Baptists in the search for biblical interpretation and theological knowledge that would contribute to conscious participation in the construction of the Kingdom of God amid a Marxist society, as ours was proclaimed. The movement declared its anti-imperialist character and its fight for the construction of Cuban socialism. Likewise, it called on the churches not to be a "countersign of the Gospel" and to work for worship that responded to Cuban tradition and culture.

From the beginning, the rejection of Baptist structures was marked. The then president of the Eastern Convention even expressed in a meeting of his board of directors, "Let them fry in their own oil. Between us and COEBAC, there is not a separation, but a total divorce".

Reverend Livio Díaz accepted to work at the Caribbean Council of Churches (CCC) and settled for several years in Kingston, Jamaica, dedicated to that work. Therefore, he asked me to take on the responsibility as the main leader of the movement. I understood that I was not prepared and that I did not have sufficient capacity to face that responsibility, but the Reverend Francisco Rodés, consulted by Livio on the matter, expressed his agreement. I accepted, against my will, motivated by love for the movement that I believed could do so much to transform the Church and make it live up to the demands of the Gospel.

The more than ten years in which I fulfilled that responsibility were of intense and feverish activity. We managed, even without having official registration in the Registry of Associations, to be recognized as members of the Council of Churches, obtain the postal franchise for *El Correo Bautista*, open a bank account, and establish fruitful and positive international relations.

Among the most relevant relationships of the COEBAC in the period in which I acted as its general secretary was the one maintained with the *American Baptist Churches* (ABC) of the United States. Its secretary for Latin America, the Reverend Víctor Mercado, visited us and met with the COEBAC secretariat on more than one occasion. From the ABC we received the first financial resources for our operation, which during its first four years had depended totally on our pockets. Another relationship worth noting was the one we had with the Caribbean Justice and Peace Project, a work area of the Quakers based in Puerto Rico.

But, the approach to the life and action of Reverend Martin Luther King Jr. that promoted COEBAC from its beginning led us to establish strong and stable working ties with the Black Theology Project of the United States. Its offices, located in the *Interchurch Center* on Riverside Drive in New York, promoted visits to our activities by black pastors and leaders from various Baptist denominations based in that northern country. Every year, COEBAC systematized a theological day of reflection on the life and work of Reverend King. Black pastors and laypeople from the United States were invited to these, some even fellow fighters of the martyr of Memphis.

The climax of the relationship with the Black Theology Project was the invitation in 1984 to the Reverend Dr. Jesse Jackson to deliver the closing message on the life and work of the Reverend Martin Luther King Jr. Jackson was at that time one of the nominees of the Democratic Party of the United States to be a candidate for the presidency of that country.

When requesting permission for Dr. Jackson to enter Cuba, we were told that the country's governmental and political authorities, and especially the president, Dr. Fidel Castro, were interested in serving such a prestigious visitor. We were pleased to see this interest and agreed to "share" the guest.

Reverend Jackson participated with Fidel in various activities in Havana. One of them, a meeting with students and professors from the capital's university, took place in the Aula Magna of the high educational center before the closing service of the Theological Day, in which the relevant North American pastor would preach. Everything was prepared for the event, invitations had been sent for the service to be held in the temple of the Methodist Church on K and 25, in the El Vedado neighborhood. Under the direction of Presbyter Lois Kroheler of the Presbyterian Church, a choir had been prepared to help in the praise. Sister Dora Valentín, wife of the rector of the Evangelical Theology Seminary in Matanzas, Dr. Sergio Arce, would be in charge of the translation. The leaders of the Council of Churches, chaired by Dr. Adolfo Ham, its executive secretary, the Reverend Raúl Suárez, and I, as general secretary of COEBAC, would be on the sidewalk of K Street to welcome the visitor and his closest companions. He did not appear at the scheduled time, but an hour and ten minutes later a loud street murmur began to be heard that increased minute by minute. We could hardly believe what we saw: Dr. Jackson was coming down the middle of the street, walking next to Fidel and surrounded by an enthusiastic and happy crowd that had followed them from the university campus for the three blocks that separated it from the Methodist church.

If the surprise of those of us who had to shake hands as a sign of welcome to the visitor on the first step of the stairs that go up to the Methodist temple was great, more impressive was Fidel's appearance in the temple. The choir that was supposed to sing the hymn Cántale a Dios, written and set to music by the young engineer Héber Romero from the Los Pinos Nuevos Church of Santa Clara, to begin the service at the entrance of Reverend Jackson, became quieter as they realized the historic moment that was being lived, and as the religious song faded away, the joy of those present increased, chanting "FIDEL, FIDEL." We were witnesses to an unusual moment in Cuban history. Fidel Castro, the only president of the country who had declared that he had no religious beliefs, was the first to participate in an evangelical service.

It was my responsibility to lead the service, which is why comrade José Ramón Fernández, then Minister of Education, indicated to me the Cuban president's interest in saying a few words of greeting to those present. We gladly agreed.

The Methodist bishop Armando Rodríguez Borges was scheduled to read the text of 1 Corinthians 12 in the Bible, where the apostle Saint Paul speaks about the different gifts. After that reading of the Scriptures, Fidel intervened. We found it interesting that he began his brief words following the message of the biblical fragment, "I do not have the capacity to make a prayer, nor do I have the capacity to make a religious speech. I think I have the ability to speak in political terms..."

COEBAC had not only managed to get a Cuban president to attend an evangelical service but to contribute to it. I had reached what, from my point of view, was the beginning of a new era in relations between the Communist Party of Cuba and the Churches based in the country. A new time of dialogue and cordial relations.

In the evening, twelve Cuban evangelical leaders were invited to a reception at the Palace of the Revolution. When four of them took a rental car on the corner of 25th and J, the taxi driver, happy but surprised, told us, "Don't you know what happened today at the church on the other block!? Fidel went to that church this afternoon. All of Havana is commenting on it."

At the Palace of the Revolution, after being received by the Cuban president, who personally shook hands and greeted the guests, we went to a room so that the foreign visitor and Fidel could respond to the journalists who were waiting for a press conference. After it was over, Dr. Jackson told Fidel, "We Christians are used to thanking God at all times and for all things, but especially when we conclude some major activity, such as our visit to Cuba and the meeting with you. Can we pray now, giving thanks?" Of course, there was no obstacle. The visitors from the United States, mostly coming from black churches in that country, began to sing hallelujah with a black spiritual rhythm, vibrant, emotional, sentimental, and profound due to the emphasis of the magnificent voices. Then, before the party and government authorities present, Dr. Jackson thanked God for everything that had happened. Perhaps it was the first time that a voice was raised publicly in prayer to the God of life in that place.

The Camps on Christian Social Responsibility carried out by COEBAC deserve special mention, from the first, held at the CANIP in Villa Clara in May 1974, to the last, held in Jagüey Grande in 1992. I consider that the first five were decisive in the formation of a movement that was born amid misunderstandings and opposition from the structures, which, without openly declaring, worked for its eradication.

The second took place at the Evangelical Theology Seminary in Matanzas. The next was on the grounds of the Yumurí Baptist Camp, property of the Baptist Convention of Western Cuba. We are still wondering how the authorization was achieved. I do not forget that I presented a work there entitled "Baptist Structures and Domination." We held the fourth in the facilities of the Episcopal Church of Camagüey, and a year later, in 1977, we met at the Second Baptist Church of Santiago de Cuba. The number of participants was much greater, and for the first time, we had the presence of a large group of young people from the Ebenezer Baptist Church of

Marianao and its pastor, the Reverend Raúl Suárez Ramos, with whom until then, we had not managed to consolidate the relationships. One of the days of this activity took place in the Baptist temple of Caney and was entirely dedicated to remembering the life and work of Frank País García. Dr. Adolfo Ham Reyes, who had been pastor of that congregation in the late 1950s, presented a tremendous quality assessment of Frank's role in the clandestine struggle against the Batista dictatorship and his always-evident commitment to faith and ecclesiastical participation. Very memorable was the presence among us on this occasion of Dr. Jean Pierre Bastian, Bible professor at the Baptist Seminary and the Theological Community of Mexico. Dr. Bastian was the first foreign personality to participate in one of our events.

But if it were a question of looking for a moment of consolidation of the COEBAC, the following camp on the social responsibility of the Christian, the sixth, held at the facilities of the Ebenezer Baptist Church in Marianao, should be noted. Despite the incomprehension of some of the members of the national secretariat of the movement, at the initiative of Pastor Luis Villalón we received, without having conditions for this, eighteen brothers and sisters from the Nordic countries. "The Swedes," as we began to call them, gave the event very special characteristics with their youth and dynamism. After the camp, which also had the presence and contribution of Dr. Luis Rivera

Pagán from Puerto Rico, they traveled to various churches in the country, promoting an understanding of the Gospel that was different from that of the majority of the churches visited but well assimilated by the charisma of the group.

An activity that took place before each national event was voluntary agricultural work. Since 1979, a group of young people, sponsored by COEBAC, worked in a place near the one selected for the national camp together with militants from the Union of Young Communists, side by side and arm in arm, giving a boost to agricultural tasks that required it, exchange experiences and get to know each other better. In addition, young Puerto Ricans and Americans sent by the Quaker Justice and Peace Project to share with us participated in these productive agricultural works.

The triumph of the Sandinista Revolution in Nicaragua on July 19, 1979, brought to Cuba a first delegation of Baptists from that country: Jerjes Ruiz, at the time rector of the Baptist Seminary of Managua; Mireya Domínguez, president of the Baptist Convention; and Sixto Ulloa, leader of the First Baptist Church of Managua. They were received by COEBAC and that was the beginning of a very fruitful and positive relationship between it and the Baptist Convention of Nicaragua. Year after year, pastors and Baptist leaders from that country traveled to ours to participate in the activities organized by our movement, and, at the same time, brigades of Cuban pastors and lay people went to Nicaragua.

Another interesting working relationship was the one signed with the Baptist Seminary of Mexico. That renowned theological institution, together with the Mexican Theological Community and the financial help of the American Baptist Convention, opened its doors for some of the leaders of the COEBAC – Adalberto Cuéllar, José Alfonso Carabeo, José Aurelio Paz, Ruth Troyano, Ángela María Hernández and Asael Corrales – studied at that institution. Thanks to the Mexican Baptist Seminary, COEBAC established relations with the Salvadoran Baptist pastor Augusto Cotto, who visited us on one occasion. Cotto later became chaplain of the Farabundo Martí National Liberation Front (FLMN). An unfortunate plane accident took his life in his youth. Despite the strong repression and the difficulty in maintaining relations with Cuba and the Cubans, the COEBAC managed to have two Salvadoran sisters present in one of its camps who, in conditions of anonymity, brought us the desire for freedom and social justice in their country. Relations with the Emmanuel Baptist Church of San Salvador existed even in the midst of the repression that that country was suffering. Thanks to the political change that occurred later, it was possible to sustain with her a stable and fraternal experience of faith and pastoral accompaniment.

Living According to the Circumstances

After eleven years as general secretary of COEBAC, I felt that the growth and scope of the movement exceeded my capacity, so I asked my colleagues to replace me. Even though they did not share my views on the matter, a year later, I managed to have Sister Gisela Pérez Muñiz assume the position. She was followed by Manuel Delgado, Moisés Figueroa, Modesto González, Lourdes Hernández and Amelia Pérez Muñiz.

As a result of the COEBAC experience, the Martin Luther King Jr. Memorial Center was founded in 1987 and then attached to the Ebenezer Baptist Church. Another indisputable fruit of the COEBAC was the official constitution, on September 8, 1989, of the Fraternity of Baptist Churches of Cuba (FIBAC), a denomination that, in its beginnings, largely channeled the struggles and aspirations of our movement. These two institutions, in addition to the B. G. Lavastida Ecumenical Center in Santiago de Cuba and the Kayros Center, attached to the First Baptist Church of Matanzas, caused the drive and dynamism of the COEBAC to diminish. Some of its most significant leaders had to use their forces in these endeavors born from the impact and creativity of the work of COEBAC. This added to other subjective factors and significantly weakened the work until, in 2007, a group of former members of the movement put it in the hands of Pastor Eduardo González.

Call To The Pastorate

Perhaps the first time someone thought that my vocation was to be a "worker of the Vineyard of the Lord" was in 1953, when I began as leader of the Union of Intermediates in the First Baptist Church of Camagüey. At that time, Dr. Gloria García Mellado, who had married the engineer Jorge Castellanos, was a counselor of the Intermediate Union. He called me one day to advise me that, at the end of the sixth grade (1954), I should enter the Secondary Education Institute to complete high school and then continue studies at the Theological Seminary of the Baptist Convention of Eastern Cuba. Jorge insisted that this was my vocation and I had to do the relevant studies.

My parents did not see the proposal favorably, especially my father considered that it was not good to jump from the sixth grade, which was ending, to the Secondary School without going through the Upper Primary School. Both he and my mother dismissed the advice that Jorge Castellanos and Gloria García Mellado had given me.

I, therefore, completed my upper primary studies, and upon completing them, my intention was to enroll in the Normal School of Teachers. My interest in theological studies did not find support from my family, who understood that I lacked the vocation for it and that the best thing I could do was study at the Business School.

Sister Nohema Carracedo, faithful member of the First Baptist Church of Camagüey, mother of Ruth, Abraham and Marta Proveyer – the first two my contemporaries and, therefore, members of the Union of Intermediates of which I was leader, and the third, a member of the same group when I was her advisor – once said at a meeting of members of the Church, I no longer remember why, "Noel is quite a pastor. He, and no one else but him, is the guide of the intermediates of this church. The one who shepherds those boys here is Noel." I remember the expression, the face, and the dynamic and strong voice with which Nohema said it. I thought, "That's really what I do: shepherd these guys." After many years I understood that being a pastor is not solely and exclusively being in charge of the spiritual guidance of a church, but rather it is guiding, especially by example, people who are in the pastor's area of influence.

The outbreak of the Cuban Revolution in 1959 completely changed the course of my life. With the arrival of the Revolution to power in January of that year, my humanist aspirations increased, and revolutionary proposals filled my mind and heart. I continued my studies at the Pinson School of the Methodist Church in Camagüey. The Professional School of Commerce had been closed due to student struggles, and I had only been able to study there for one year. Pinson was a magnificent student-teacher entity. I felt very fulfilled in it, and I stood out a lot in the Bible classes and in the religious services that we gave at the San Pablo Methodist Church, attached to the school, in the La Zambrana neighborhood of the city of Camagüey.

At the conclusion of the National Literacy Campaign some of my close friends from the Baptist Church entered the Baptist Seminary in a course that began in January 1962, and I was tempted to apply, but I did not want to leave my secular job. At that time, I was a teacher within the Revolutionary Armed Forces, and I felt very happy to be able to teach to rebel soldiers who required it. I would have liked to be a worker priest, like those in France, about whom I had read a lot, but to study at the Baptist Seminary of Santiago de Cuba, I had to leave everything and enroll.

Years of many occupations and worries followed. The traditional pastorate, from my point of view, was not compatible with the pressing tasks of a country in revolution. On the other hand, the Church would not have accepted a pastor busy with secular tasks, so I had to give up the dream of being a "worker priest."

When, in 1978, we were separated from the membership of the First Baptist Church of Ciego de Ávila, the call to the pastorate became present. We had to pastor the more than

Living According to the Circumstances

twenty people separated from the membership of that congregation. It was then that we began regular meetings of prayer, meditation, and adoration of the Lord, sometimes at the house of Ormara's grandmother, Estefanía Machado, other times at her parents' house or at ours. It was not only the collective worship of the Lord, the study of the Word and prayers that was demanded of the group, for whose coordination I assumed responsibility but the visitation and spiritual guidance that was required, especially in the midst of a confrontation that so much damaged us all and required a lot of effort to continue loving the Church despite the marginalization suffered. That group was consolidated, and the frequency of the meetings of what would later become the Emmanuel Baptist Church grew and became more and more part of our needs.

The beginning of missionary activity in central Bolivia on February 5, 1992, awakened my dormant pastoral vocation. For the first time, I felt fulfilled as a pastor. Later, we began missionary work in Colorado on Friday afternoons and evenings. On Sunday mornings I traveled there to visit, to encourage, to console, to teach. The missions of Colorado and Bolivia gave me the strength to fight, even though I was still working as an average technician in the reading area for blind and low-vision people at the Provincial Library. At last, I was a working priest. Ormara and I traveled to Bolivia on Saturdays and sometimes another day of the week, not many times, for transportation reasons. Colorado and Bolivia were the two pastoral training schools in which my vocation was outlined and developed.

On the other hand, the existing congregation in Ciego de Ávila wanted to organize itself with more consistency, and in mid-1992, it adopted the agreement to hold activities every Sunday at four in the afternoon. I joyfully assumed the responsibility of also being the guide of that group, which, for obvious reasons, required much more attention and capacity than the missions in Bolivia and Colorado.

On November 13, 1994, after a beautiful council, the Emmanuel Baptist Church was established, which officially named me its pastor. A year later, on March 26, 1995, by agreement of the church, the Examining and Guiding Council was established, which, once its approval was given, ordained me to the Holy Ministry in an unforgettable liturgical celebration held in my mother's house, where we lived, and which we had converted into what was then called a "house of worship."

I have very good memories of that council in which experienced pastors asked me important questions. One of them, whose name I prefer to silence, tried to put me on the spot by inquiring about my views regarding baptism. He wanted me to affirm that the only valid baptism is that performed by immersion, as Baptist tradition generally assumes. I tried to explain that the important thing about baptism is not its form but its symbolism: death, burial, and life. But the aforementioned pastor did not accept, "as Baptists that we are," that opinion about "something of such importance to the denomination." Thank God, there were people like Francisco Rodés and Adalberto Cuéllar at the council who knew what I meant and what baptism really means for those who wish to give public testimony of their commitment to the Lord. In the end, with the aforementioned pastor's vote against me, I was approved and ordained to the Holy Ministry.

Pastoring is not an easy task, although it is glorious. I think all my colleagues in the ministry can agree with me that it is a complicated task. On occasions, I have been asked if it is easy to shepherd when blind, and my answer has always been, "It is not easy at all, it's complicated. But is it easy for those who are not?"

If indelible was the liturgical celebration in which I was ordained to the ministry, just as great but loaded with deep nostalgia was my emotion the day I preached my last sermon as active pastor of the Emmanuel Baptist Church of Ciego de Ávila. It was Sunday, May 24, 2009, just one week after the installation of Eduardo González Hernández as pastor of our church. It is impossible for me to describe the set of feelings, memories and evaluations that I experienced in each moment of that celebration, but I must say that it was a day in which all the sensations and emotions came together. I had managed, by the grace of Jesus Christ, to embrace for several years a vocation that perhaps I had not ventured into before due to my indomitable character.

If you asked me what my first experience was as pastor of a congregation, I would have to tell what I experienced at the Baptist Church of Guáimaro. The Reverend Luis Villalón Rubio and his wife, Dinorah Mata del Río, also a graduate of the Baptist Seminary of Eastern Cuba, had received a scholarship to study abroad. The congregation in Guáimaro could not be left without a pastor for an entire course and asked Ormara and me to fill in for him.

Ormara was studying for her Philology degree at the Marta Abreu Central University of Santa Clara. She had to attend classes every other week and returned home on Saturday night. It was a powerful reason not to accept Luis and Dinorah's request. Ormara and I talked. I must say that I was eager to undertake such a beautiful task, but I understood that it would be very complicated for her to travel from Santa Clara to Guáimaro on Saturday and then, on Sunday night, return to Ciego de Ávila. Keep in mind that from Santa Clara to Guáimaro there are about 370 kilometers, and that, although there are buses that pass through the place, there is no direct route between both points. On the other hand, the central train passes far from Guáimaro. It makes a stop in Martí, about twenty kilometers away, and another in Palo Seco, a little closer.

Living According to the Circumstances

Ormara accepted the challenge gladly and bravely. It was a beautiful experience, not only because I was a pastor for the first time but also because the church accepted us with great affection and encouraged us to move forward. Since my childhood I knew the church of Guáimaro, which was even attended on some occasions by my pastor, the Reverend Rafael Gregorich. It was a very small congregation with very few leaders, but the pastoral work of Villalón and his wife raised that congregation, which lived the experience of what, in religious language, especially Protestant or evangelical, we know as a revival. I think it is important to highlight that Pastor Villalón not only pastorally attended to that congregation but also those of Elia, Martí, Miraflores, San Carlos, and another one whose name I do not remember. Of course, it was totally impossible for me to take care of those other congregations, working – as I did then – as an accountant at the Higher Agricultural Institute of Ciego de Ávila. Fortunately, Villalón had managed to get their brothers of the church to come to Guáimaro at least once a month, which constituted an opportunity to encourage them, listen to them and guide them. Guáimaro was a tremendous school of pastoral training, especially at a time when we were experiencing the ostracism produced by our separation from the membership of the First Baptist Church of Ciego de Ávila.

I remember that shortly after my election as pastor, I spoke with a great friend, also a pastor, Elmer Lavastida Alfonso, and I said to him, "Elmer, I have waited so long to accept this call from God! I think I kicked against the sting."

He replied consolingly, "God has time for each task and for each person. Now it has been your Kairos."

Living According to the Circumstances

The Emmanuel Baptist Church

Perhaps in other denominations, it is different, but for those of us who were born in a Baptist congregation, it is not easy to abandon that tradition. In the case of Ormara and me, this has been the case.

We were forced to stop participating in the responsibilities of the Baptist Convention of Eastern Cuba first, and then even of membership in the First Baptist Church of Ciego de Ávila, from which, as I have already said, we were separated. The time we had the responsibility of helping in the pastorate of the Guáimaro Baptist Church (August 1984-May 1985) reaffirmed our love for the work of our elders.

The impossibility of being part of the Baptist congregation of Ciego de Ávila prompted us, as I have already told, to give help to the Methodist Church. But we, and especially my in-laws, did not find there what we had lost. It was then that we decided to increase family meetings of gathering and worship on Sunday nights. These were carried out mainly in the house of Estefanía Machado, Ormara's grandmother, and sporadically in her parents' house until we managed to systematize them in ours, located at 423 on Chicho Valdés Street.

Christmas, Easter, the Vigil awaiting the new year, Mother's Day, and other traditional celebrations were part of the meetings of a family group in which other people sometimes participated.

Living According to the Circumstances

We collectively decided that every Sunday at four in the afternoon, we would meet in our house to worship the Lord and study his Word. At first, it was the continuity of a family encounter with the Lord, but others joined us. First, those who, like us, had lost their membership in the First Church and then other guests.

The group became so large that we had to change the meeting place three times. From the informality of a family gathering, we moved to a well-structured liturgical celebration with all the parts that we understood and understood it should have. At the same time, we had begun missionary work, first in central Bolivia and later in the town of Colorado.

At the end of 1992 we had a group of new converts prepared and willing to receive baptism. They were: Carmen Barreto, Pedro Gutiérrez, Rafael Almeida, Zoila Sánchez, Rafael Cepero, Pablo Ulloa, Jose R. Mejías and Eddy Bravo. They were baptized in the Majagua River on September 4, 1994, by the Reverend Adalberto Cuéllar and constituted the embryo of a congregation to which we would join sisters and brothers who came from the First Church. They were: Alicia Cao, José M. Nolla, Ormara Nolla, Loida Nolla, José A. Paz, María Collot, Gabriela Rodríguez, Iris Oliva, María M. del Rio and me.

The Sunday celebratory meetings were filled with more and more people interested in the emergence of a new congregation, which made us decide that it was necessary to give proper organization to the incipient church. We started conversations with some members of the Board of Directors of the Baptist Convention of Eastern Cuba, but they rejected our request to be recognized as a church affiliated with it. Although we planned to talk with the directors of the Western Convention, we did not manage to do so since we understood that if those who had always known us were not able to receive us, even less would those who barely knew of our testimony and action.

The Fraternity of Baptist Churches of Cuba (FIBAC) was already a reality, and it had been joined by the group of believers who met at Elia Fonseca's house in Bayamo, who had had an experience as painful as ours when they had been separated from the First Baptist Church of that city.

Not all of us who met as a Baptist congregation were in favor of applying for membership in the Fraternity. It took us almost two years to reach a majority agreement. Obviously, there was no other alternative, and even though it didn't seem like the best option, we had no other way out.

The FIBAC did not reject our application for membership, and on November 13, 1994, the Examining and Guiding Council for the constitution of the Emmanuel Baptist Church was held at our premises, attended by pastors Adalberto Cuéllar, Ena García, Clara Rodés, Francisco Rodés, and Remberto Ortiz. That same afternoon, we held the liturgical celebration that sealed with great joy the approval obtained by the examining board. I had the privilege that very day of being chosen by the nascent church as its pastor and of naming the church Emmanuel. On the third Sunday, we began to carry out our activities in a place at the back of the patio that we called the chapel, and which constituted a magnificent space for worship. That covered place, with appropriate chairs and an electric keyboard, became the desired temple, where we even held communion services and even a wedding.

On March 26, 1995, by agreement of the church, a new council was constituted, this time for my ordination to the Holy Ministry. It was made up of the reverends Remberto Ortiz, Lázaro Cuesta, Adalberto Cuéllar, and Francisco Rodés.

The premises became too small for us, and we began to dream first, to work later, and to always pray to achieve the official acquisition of a new premises. Of course, we did not have the financial resources for this, but we did have a great sense of urgency and hope. We began conversations with the official of the Office of Attention to Religious Affairs of the Provincial Committee of the Communist Party, Mr. Omar Martínez, who would later be a great friend and a servant of the church from his partisan position. He, in turn, sought guidance in this regard and we soon began the search for a suitable location that we would buy with official authorization, which at

Living According to the Circumstances

that time was achieved on a case-by-case basis and with many bureaucratic procedures.

The house located on Joaquín de Agüero on the corner of Abraham Delgado, today the Catholic bishopric of the diocese of Ciego de Ávila, was for sale. After visiting it, it seemed like a suitable place. The price was high, but it was worth it, not only for the building but also for the land at the back. A week later, we completed the procedures to purchase the premises, along with the actions to get the FIBAC to help us obtain the necessary resources. After various bureaucratic procedures, we managed to place the purchase file on the bureau of the president of the Provincial Assembly of People's Power, who had to certify that the government of the province had no interest in the acquisition of that building, given that the government is, by law, the first buyer of any property in its district. We spent a year waiting for the signature. One day, unexpectedly, they announced to us that the seller had removed the file from the office of the president of the Provincial Assembly of People's Power. We did not know the cause, until we found out that the bishop of the diocese of the Catholic Church was in the process of unofficially purchasing the house, which happened.

That fact, which upset us a lot, forced us to start the process from scratch a second time. After much searching, we found that the house of Libertad 167, where our church is located today, was for sale. We visited it, and although we thought it was inferior to the previous one, we accepted the seller's offer and started the required process again.

It took us eleven long months to get official approval for the purchase of the home that we would convert into a temple. Once that legal requirement was obtained, we lacked the financial resources. FIBAC had given us three-quarters of the money needed. It was then that we requested a loan from the Council of Churches of Cuba to cover the difference. We were granted the loan, to be paid in one year. We were not able to make the payment on the established date, which caused us great concern because we had compromised our word. Providentially, during a visit to our congregation by the Rev. Stan Hastey, then executive director of the Alliance of Baptists of North America, he learned of our concern. Two months later, he informed us that a Baptist pastor in the United States from a church affiliated with the Alliance had received as a retirement gift an amount of money of which he wanted to donate half for missionary work. The amount that came to us through Reverend Hastey was exactly what we required to settle our debt to the Council.

On September 15, 1996, we dedicated to the Lord the building that today is our house of prayer. The liturgical celebration of blessing of the building was attended by the Very Reverend Pablo Odén Marichal, an Episcopal priest who at that time also served as president of the Council of Churches of Cuba; Sister Xiomara Arenas of the Presbyterian Church and vice president of the CIC; comrade Efrén Pérez Gómez, delegate of the Popular Power constituency where the church is located; and Mr. Omar Martínez, from the Office of Attention to Religious Affairs of the Provincial Committee of the PCC. The then small sanctuary was filled with jubilant and grateful brothers and sisters in an unforgettable liturgical celebration. God answered to our prayers.

A year later, a group of Alcoholics Anonymous (AA) was started in that place, the first in the province of Ciego de Ávila, and almost in parallel, a program began that held pastoral care sessions for the elderly every Thursday, which received the name of The Golden Age.

In December 1997, we began a task – which we have continued – consisting of gathering clothing and accessories for newborn babies in a basket that is delivered every December 25 to the first infant who in need is born that day. The delivery at the hospital has become a celebration in which a small delegation from the church, health personnel, and the mothers present participate. Emmanuel's large family enjoys contributing resources to this noble endeavor.

Two other community outreach efforts were: The Good Samaritan Storeroom and the Sewing Workshop. Due to the lack of linen items in the city's hospitals during the so-called

Special Period, two sisters designated by our congregation, Alicia and Lucinda Cao Machado, lent sheets, pillowcases, towels, housecoats, and other items to those who needed them due to a hospital admission. The items were returned at the end of the hospital stay, and those sisters were in charge of keeping them in excellent condition for a new loan. This work extended from 1996 to 2001.

The other social service activity has been the sewing workshop. A group of sisters, first under the leadership of Mary Terry, then Berta López, then Blanca Gómez, and later Xiomara Gutiérrez, meets weekly. With fabrics and other items donated by foreign visitors, they made housecoats, pajamas and other items for women in the congregation who need them, elderly women from other churches, women in maternity homes, and elderly people in specialized facilities. They also made clothing for children within the missions established by Emmanuel in various places in the province. Several times a year, led by the women of the sewing workshop, a Talent Fair is held in which the low-cost sale of items made in the workshop is highly demanded by Emmanuel's large family. The resources acquired at the fair are used to finance the workshop or for other purposes determined by the church itself.

In 1997, work began on the creation of a library specialized in matters related to religion, serving secular researchers, the city's religious leaders, and Emmanuel's large family. Significant is the collection of Bibles of different translations, versions and formats.

A room in the building became the church office and, at the same time, that of the Pastoral Program for People with Disabilities of the Council of Churches of Cuba. As part of the ecumenical feeling of the congregation, from the very beginning of Emmanuel's activity in the new location, the temple and its rooms serve for meetings of other congregations that need it.

Little by little, the building underwent modifications to adapt it to the requirements. Following the guidelines of the local Heritage office, the eclecticism of the front and the temple was preserved, which is maintained even when enlarged. Offices, classrooms, library, bedrooms, sewing room, and warehouses were added according to needs and possibilities. Given my manifest inability to carry out construction tasks, and at my request, Brother Eduardo González Hernández, who would later become pastor of the church, took care of everything related to both the official procedures and the expansion and remodeling tasks and adaptation of the premises.

As a Baptist tradition, the Sunday School existed from the very beginning of the congregation, even before we were established as a church. In the new location, with more facilities, classes were expanded.

Living According to the Circumstances

It is worth mentioning that the following people did theological studies in our congregation: Rafael Almeida, later pastor of the Gethsemane Church in Colorado, affiliated with the FIBAC; Abel Cotelo, pastor of an English-speaking congregation of the United Church in the United States located in the city of Miami; Pablo Ulloa, who first worked with Los Pinos Nuevos and is currently a pastor in the Reformed Episcopal Church; Illobis González, pastor of the Moravian Church in Miami; Dafne del Risco, who has worked for several years in the Music Ministry in a Presbyterian Church in Puerto Rico, and currently ordained to the Holy Ministry, she works as a Lutheran pastor in Chicago, United States; Eduardo González, the current pastor of Emmanuel and formerly of the Canaán Church in the municipality of Bolivia; and Francisco Agüero Gómez, who after graduating from the Evangelical Theology Seminary in Matanzas stopped participating in the life of the church.

Another significant achievement of Emmanuel was the establishment of missionary work in eighteen places in the province, from which the churches of Bolivia, Chambas, Colorado, Corojo, Pesquería, and La Ilusión were born.

The first visit to Emmanuel by a group from the Alliance of North American Baptists was made in June 1994. They included the Rev. Dr. Welton Gaddy, Craig Henry, D. H. Clark, and Delores Lindsay, all members of the Northminster Church from

Monroe, Louisiana. They had traveled to Cuba with the intention of finding a congregation that would satisfy their congregation's interests in establishing a brotherhood pact. Upon meeting us and after deep discussions, they rejected the continuing route projected by FIBAC, which included churches in Camagüey, Holguín, and Bayamo. They understood, and so they stated that Emmanuel would be their sister church. In the official talks to conclude the agreement, both parties agreed that we had many things in common and many more to add through the efforts that we would make together. At the time of writing these lines, twenty-four years have passed since that agreement, and relations, after temporarily diminishing, grow year after year.

The visit to our congregation by the Reverend Miguel Tomás Castro, from the Emmanuel Baptist Church, from San Salvador, El Salvador, led us to sign a twinning agreement with that church, which, with its vigorous work, had stood out in the construction of the Kingdom of God amid indescribable social and political difficulties. It was a twinning pact looking south. Subsequently, Ormara and I had the privilege of visiting them and later, the Reverend Eduardo González, already pastor of Emmanuel, did so too.

Another interesting relationship abroad is the one we have maintained since 2010 with the Congregational Church of Minneapolis, Minnesota. Its pastor, Jeff Saltari, who visited us at the first opportunity, told us about a church busy making possible the achievement of justice amid inequality and the abandonment of the most dispossessed in its society. Sister Nancy Albrecht is from that church, who for five years, has come for a month to give impetus to the Emmanuel Sewing Workshop.

I believe that my pastorate in Emmanuel, with the characteristics and ecumenical profile of our congregation, provided me with an opportunity to serve much greater than the blessing that a church in Ciego de Ávila could have provided me. I concluded my pastorate in May 2009, when the Church installed Eduardo González Hernández as pastor upon my request to cease active service. The process that the church followed for the pastoral change was very appropriate and within the best Baptist tradition. All pastors of churches affiliated with FIBAC were written and invited to be candidates for the pastorate of Emmanuel. Only Sister Dámaris Oms, a recent graduate of the Evangelical Theology Seminary in Matanzas, responded. The church, for its part, invited as possible candidates the Reverend Ramona Matos, the then-pastor Sergio Troyano, and Pastor Milagros Pérez, the last two graduates of that same seminary. Unfortunately, none of them accepted the candidacy.

At the time of the search process for candidates for the pastorate of Emmanuel, Brother Eduardo González was serving as pastor of the Canaán Baptist Church in Bolivia, affiliated with

Living According to the Circumstances

FIBAC. The Commission that was in charge of pastoral replacement invited him to be, along with Dámaris Oms, a candidate for the pastorate. In the elections held on March 10, 2009, Pastor González obtained all the votes cast except for two people. In an emotional and well-attended ceremony held in our temple on Sunday, May 31, 2009, the second pastor of our congregation was installed.

The Reverend Eduardo Gonzalez began studying Theology at the Perkins School of Theology, in Dallas, Texas, which he requested to receive in English with the aim of perfecting that language. For five summers, he traveled to the United States until he acquired a degree in Theology. Subsequently, he studied for a master's in Theology at the Evangelical Theology Seminary in Matanzas, an academic degree that he did not obtain for not submitting the thesis within the established time.

Emmanuel gained a lot from the presence of a young pastor, well prepared and with a tremendous capacity for work. His main gift as a pastor is that of the word. Every Sunday, he delivers a vibrant, contextual, polemical, and profound sermon. His pleasant manner with everyone and his friendliness make him a recipient of the affection of what we have called the great family of Emmanuel, made up of members, visitors, their relatives, and the community in general. During the pastorate of Eduardito, as we usually call him, relations with friendly and sister churches abroad were intensified, and new buildings were added.

In 2013, the church acquired the house that was owned by Sister María Collot and which she left in her will to her son. That property, with a large, constructed surface and surrounding land, has since become the Community Center of the Emmanuel Baptist Church, where the Alcoholics Anonymous program meets, recreational activities of the church are carried out, different programs operate, and it is a meeting place for Emmanuel's large family.

I have said on many occasions that if a social, religious, political, or economic cataclysm marked the end of Emmanuel's existence, we would thank God because he more than fulfilled his purpose and opened a new intention of service and a new expression of the faith, not known before in the city. On the other hand, during its existence, "angels" sent by the Lord have adorned it with love, ability, and dedication, whose actions among us are indelible.

Missionary Work

The First Baptist Church of Camagüey, where I attended since my birth, was, without a doubt, a church with a broad missionary spirit. During the pastorate of Reverend Rafael Gregorich Escalona (1934-1967), the "site of his cabin" extended beyond the city to Martí, Florida, Vertientes, and

Cromo, among other places. However, the most relevant thing in that task was the work that he did in the churches then called Haitian, to which he dragged the entire congregation. In that period, there were two conventions of Haitian churches in the territory occupied by the then Baptist Convention of Eastern Cuba: the Haitian Baptist Convention of the East and the Haitian Baptist Convention of Camagüey. The latter with more than twenty churches and missions in the vast plain of Camagüey.

Pastor Gregorich attended to them systematically: weddings, baptisms, and the Lord's Supper, among other activities, were always on his personal work agenda. It was not easy. The conditions of extreme poverty in which the men and women from that fellow country and their families lived made it very difficult to stay for several days on their properties, as Gregorich did. But we enjoyed the joy that he brought to church on his return. On many occasions, I witnessed how his faithful and hardworking wife, Consuelo Sánchez Paneque, scolded him due to the extreme expenditure of time and energy that this missionary work entailed. "Don't you realize that you're not healthy enough to do this job? Why don't the younger pastors do it?" Gregorich, with his usual calm and meekness, smiled at her and simply said, "Consuelo, it is my vocation."

Another significant missionary aspect of what was my first church were the neighborhood missions and Sunday schools. In the second half of the 1950s, we attended more than fifteen missions and Sunday schools in surrounding neighborhoods of the city: Reparto Batista (later Cándido González), Buenavista, Bellavista, Florat, Las Mercedes, Garrido, Versalles, Agramonte, Piedra Imán, Nadales, Porvenir, San Miguelito, and others. Some of us who made up the Intermediate Union Group started out in missionary work. First, we did a marathon route on our bicycles that started in Florat and continued through Piedra Imán, Agramonte, Garrido, and concluded in Versalles. We traveled through the entire city from north to west and ended in the east. With the maturity that we gained in this task, David Gregorich assumed full responsibility at Florat, and I was in charge of the work at Piedra Imán.

This last neighborhood is located a few meters from the West Central Highway after passing the elevated railway line to Santa Cruz del Sur. We entered through the street where Agroquim (the company that produces chemical fertilizers for agriculture) was located. Sunday School started at three in the afternoon, but Lucy Nieves Ramírez and I arrived much earlier to visit the neighborhood. There were many houses we went to, one week some houses and others the next week. In several of them they were already waiting for us and asked us to pray for one situation or another, a moment that we also took advantage of to read a piece of Scripture and leave a message. Then, at the house of sister Carmen Gutiérrez and her husband, Nelson

Barrameda, the activities were carried out. Lucy was in charge of the adult class, and I was in charge of the children's class. The growth of the Sunday School prompted us to rent a house in front of it where the children met while the adult classes were held in the living room of the Barrameda-Gutiérrez home. A few months later, we decided to hold services every Thursday night. I remember one that we celebrated on the occasion of Holy Week, that was attended by more than a hundred adults. For health reasons, Sister Lucy could not continue the work, and it was then that Sister Nena San José began to collaborate in this activity. The three daughters of the Barrameda-Gutiérrez couple, Carmen, Eloísa, and Arelis, as well as their little brother, Nelson, helped a lot in the progress of that mission.

Piedra Imán was my first missionary school. With Lucy first, then with Nena, I learned a lot. The two differed in styles, interpretations of faith, and biblical-theological training, and both constituted two aspects of my missionary training process. What to say, how to act in each visit according to the interests of the families visited, how to encourage, exhort, and form new converts: I learned all this on the go and at a very young age because I began that work when I was only fifteen years old, and I continued until I was eighteen. Many Sundays were dedicated to traveling to Ciego de Ávila to visit Ormara, who was already my girlfriend.

Living According to the Circumstances

When we moved to Ciego de Ávila in 1968, I was nostalgic for the missionary life of what was until then my church. The First Baptist Church of Ciego de Ávila did not have the same missionary zeal as that of Camagüey. In the aforementioned period, there was only missionary work in the Maidique neighborhood, a work that fell mainly to my mother-in-law, Alicia Cao Machado, and in which her daughters helped, especially Loida. I remember having discussed the situation on more than one occasion with the pastor of the church, the Reverend Gilberto Prieto Socarás, who would have greatly liked to enroll in that task, but the objective reality was that the times did not make it feasible to start a missionary work. Lack of understanding about the work of the church was at an all-time high. Neither in Ciego de Ávila nor in any other part of the country were there favorable conditions for missionary work.

From the previous pastorate, that of Reverend Marino Santos Martínez, the church maintained a mission in Stewart Sugar Mill, today Venezuela, which became a church under the pastorate of Reverend Prieto in 1969. It was also interesting that when the town of Sanguily, southwest of Ciego de Ávila, the first peasant settlement built by the Revolution, with optimal conditions for their lives, a Sunday Bible School was started there. Every Sunday afternoon, the pastor or the deacon Ramón Echevarría took the sisters Nora Hernández and Ormara Nolla in the car owned by the church to attend to the work that was carried out in the portal of the local primary school. Unfortunately, this incipient missionary work ceased due to the circumstances of incomprehension characteristic of the time.

The rebirth of my missionary activity occurred in a very special way. On the afternoon of February 5, 1992, I gave a presentation on the history of the evangelical churches in the province of Ciego de Ávila to party leaders of the province at the headquarters of the Provincial Committee of the Communist Party, in which the ideologue of the party in Bolivia curiously asked why there was no evangelical or Protestant church in that territory. Upon returning home, a very dear colleague from the National Association of the Blind, who at the time was its president in Bolivia, Idonelis Espinosa, called me by phone.

Very distressed and depressed by the prevailing situation in the country – we were then living in what was called the Special Period – she told me of her concern and sadness, her restlessness and sorrow, "Imagine that I have the child without diapers, we cannot find adequate food, I remember my grandmother saying when I was a girl, and things were bad that we didn't worry and trust in the Lord. Does that mean anything to you? It doesn't say anything to me." Idonelis was a member of the Communist Youth. I had met her about five years before on a tour in which I accompanied the president of the Association of the Blind of the province, Luis Guardarrama, through the municipality of Bolivia. That day we arrived at the town of Liborio, where they had told us that there was a family in which there were some people with low vision.

It wasn't difficult for us to find Idonelis's parents' house, and she, sitting in a modest armchair, was listening to a radio program from the provincial station, Radio Surco, very popular at that time, called Once Variedades las Once. Idonelis, who had a magnificent musical ear, sang what she was listening to in very good tune, and louder than the radio. Thanks to the efforts of the ANCI, she found a job as a general assistant in the Municipal Labor Sector, but her intelligence, industriousness, and determination led her to work first as a room staff and later as a specialist in the Municipal Museum.

The conversation with Idonelis that day in February 1992 concluded when she said to me, "Why don't you come to Cunagua to tell some of my friends those things that you have told me?" And then she added, "In Bolivia, there are many people of goodwill who would like to listen to you."

Exactly a week later, I got off the bus at the micro-district stop to go to Idonelis and her husband Miguelito's house. Her phone call had been an invitation that was impossible to refuse: being able to speak about the hope of Jesus Christ to people who had never heard that message before was something that could not be put off. My friend welcomed me with a contagious joy, characteristic of her, and explained to me that her friends

Living According to the Circumstances

were waiting for us in Vallina, a peripheral community of the town, at Juana Ester Pérez's house. Juana was a very beloved woman in the population, the sweets she made were desired by everyone, there was no celebration in Bolivia that did not have Juana Ester's sweets in its toast, and the best of all is that she very rarely wanted to collect them. But as a result of her diabetes, she had gone blind, and from that moment on, she had confined herself to her bedroom. "For me, life is over, I have nothing to do without sight," was her lament.

That February 10, seven mutual friends of Idonelis and her, all living near her, met in the dining room of Juana Ester Pérez's house. Juana Ester said that she left her room to be able to attend to the visitor that "he can actually understand me well because he is also blind." I remember that the key text of that sermon, which was more of a conversation, was based on the words of Jesus Christ recorded in the Gospel according to Saint John in chapter 10, verse 10, "I am come that they might have life, and that they might have it more abundantly." The message of the Word reached those who heard it, but especially to the hostess, who later said many times, "I was born to a new life that afternoon."

From that first visit, there were others every week. Saturday was the day chosen for the periodic meetings of what would later become the Canaan Baptist mission of the Vallina community in Cunagua. Juana dressed in her best clothes and, with some of her neighbors, she went out to invite, early in the morning, for the service that would take place at four in the afternoon at her house. The mission grew not only numerically but also in knowledge of the Word and in responsibility.

Juana Ester became ill due to her uncontrolled diabetes. She was confined in the provincial hospital of Camagüey and had to suffer an amputation. She went to the room singing and encouraging the doctors and paramedical staff who attended to her. These showed their surprise and bewilderment at having as a patient a woman so expressive, happy, and hopeful for the future, whatever it may be. Juana left to be with the Lord unexpectedly. Her funeral in Bolivia was a demonstration of mourning by the entire population. The teachers dismissed the students early so they could go to the funeral service that had been announced. Commercial establishments closed their doors or opened them later. Virtually the entire town crowded inside and outside the local funeral home. I did not have the privilege of being present. That task had to be carried out by my wife, Ormara, who had never had to face such an experience. She did an excellent job, and the Lord gave her the exact and necessary words.

Six months after starting the missionary work in Bolivia, a friend, also blind and leader of the ANCI in the province, but who had his family in the town of Colorado, municipality of Baraguá, invited me to go preach at the house of Juana María

Ramírez. He told me that the First Baptist Church of Ciego de Ávila and its then pastor, the Reverend Melvin Puebla Rodríguez, had visited that house and held meetings with some regularity, but that for three months, no one had taken care of that task and some of the people who had known the Lord wanted to continue and systematize the meetings.

When I first visited the house, there were about eight or nine people there. Three of them had ties to Baptist churches in the eastern provinces where they came from. After praying and singing, I offered them the help of my modest efforts to visit them, pray, and share the Word if they had no ties with the church that had previously visited them and desired our presence in the place. They all stated that our missionary action would be convenient for them because they had not sensed the solidarity and continuity of the pastoral action that they required. That was the beginning of the Gethsemane Baptist mission, converted into a Baptist church of the same name on November 12, 1996.

It is essential to mention the zeal and love for the work of a local couple, he Haitian and she the daughter of a father and mother born in that sister nation. Salomón and Clara were an inspiration for our lives. The simplicity and humility of their work, his zeal and responsibility towards the church, and the detachment and selflessness of his conduct filled Ormara and me with responsibility and enthusiasm.

Living According to the Circumstances

Both the Bolivian and Colorado missions had been born and developed without the Emmanuel Baptist Church having yet been established. While each week we traveled to both places to pray together, praise the Lord, and share the Word, meetings of the same meaning in Ciego de Ávila were not held with the same regularity as those in Bolivia and Colorado.

After Sunday services were systematized in our house at the beginning of 1993, a young man, Pablo Ulloa Doña, who was part of the first group baptized in the nascent church, showed his interest in studying Theology in the Seminary. I did not feel motivated to agree to his request, I did not see in Brother Ulloa a marked pastoral vocation. He had known the Lord in the church of the Assemblies of God, but then he had been related to the Episcopal Church, from which he came to our activities, he attended classes for new converts and was baptized by the Reverend Adalberto Cuéllar. A visit to Emmanuel by the Reverend Clara Rodés, then president of the Fraternity of Baptist Churches of Cuba, made me modify my criteria. She suggested that to check him out and give him the opportunity to demonstrate his vocation.

Since Ulloa was residing at that time in the municipality of Florencia, I told him, "Look, Pablo, Chambas is one of the largest and most populated municipalities in this province. In its territory, there is only one evangelical church, the Church of God in Punta Alegre. In Chambas, there were two churches of

Living According to the Circumstances

Los Pinos Nuevos, one in the municipal seat and the other in Falla, but for reasons unknown to me, both disappeared; even Chambas, which had its own premises, apparently lost it. Show me your missionary and pastoral vocation by initiating visits to the place and exploring the possibility of holding regular meetings".

Two months after that conversation, on December 7, 1994, in the home of Zelmira Caraballo, we held the first meeting of what would be the Betania Baptist mission, established as a church on June 3, 2007. That missionary work that was carried out with weekly visits to the place, generally accompanied by Ormara, suffered a strong division.

Relations with Ulloa deteriorated due to his excessive material interest. Complaints in this sense and his lack of understanding of the value of dedication, sacrifice, and selflessness distanced him from the work that he had so rightly begun. It was then that the Evangelical Association of Los Pinos Nuevos hired him to carry out missionary work in Chambas itself. I remember talking to the president of that work, who was concerned about the method used and assured me that this was not the practice of his denomination. However, Brother Ulloa began to hold weekly services, even in the place where we met. That duplicity, not at all convenient, led me to change locations. The mission was divided, as in Corinth according to the letter of Saint Paul, between "those of Paul and those of Noel." It was an extremely painful and sad experience.

Months later, when Pablo Ulloa and his wife, also converted by Emmanuel's actions, began to study at the Evangelical Seminary of Los Pinos Nuevos, a new missionary from that denomination arrived in Chambas, and with him, the work of the mission was strengthened, which even recovered its lost premises. In the end, we thanked God because instead of one preaching point, there were two in Chambas. From the initial contribution, in that town where there was no missionary work and the restart of the work of Los Pinos Nuevos, other denominations were then able to arrive, and they have established themselves and continued the proclamation of the Word.

Bolivia, Colorado, and Chambas were the seeds of the missionary work of the Emmanuel Baptist Church, which I began to officially pastor after its constitution in November 1994, but they were not the only missionary experiences in the territory. Guasimales was also on the border of the province of Camagüey with Ciego de Avila. Corojo later converted into the La Vid Verdadera Baptist Church. Pachi, Gaspar, Baraguá, El Centro, Contingente, Clementina (all from the Baraguá municipality), and Pesquería converted into the Koinonia church on October 24, 2014. The head of the municipality of Ciro Redondo and La Ilusión, the latter converted in 2010 into the

Gabaón Baptist church, both in the Ciro Redondo municipality. And we also carry out missionary work in the Canaleta district of Ciego de Ávila, in the city of Morón, in Liborio (Bolivia), and in Quesada and Navarra (in the municipality of Ciego de Ávila). All those places learned of the message of life and hope of Jesus Christ through our actions.

It is worth highlighting that the extensive missionary work that I carried out during my pastorate in the province of Ciego de Ávila was possible thanks to the collaboration of several people. First of all, Ormara. Not yet retiring from her job at the Provincial Library, she accompanied me in her free time to some of those places. I remember very especially the many times we went to Bolivia and Chambas together. Both missionary activities took place on Saturdays, Bolivia at four in the afternoon and Chambas at eight-thirty at night. Ormara left work at noon, and at one in the afternoon she was behind the wheel of our car to drive the seventy kilometers that separate us from Bolivia. Then, at the end of the liturgical celebration there, she traveled another seventy kilometers to Chambas (Ciego de Ávila, Bolivia, and Chambas practically form an equilateral triangle).

Many times, in order not to cause expenses to the brothers of the mission, we would stop near Puente Grande, and we would eat bread with something we were carrying, and we would have a juice or yogurt. This frugal dinner was later replaced by the one we began to have at Neysi Quintero's house in Chambas. It was at her home where, at that time, we carried out mission activities. From Chambas, we returned to Ciego de Ávila, generally around ten at night. The rush, plus the hustle and bustle in those two places, forced Ormara, already around eleven at night, to make a stop at the entrance to the town of Ciro Redondo on the road that leads to Peonía to sleep for ten minutes, with which, incredibly, was replenished and we continued the trip.

Ormara was not only a driver but also a pianist because we carried the electric keyboard with us. All that changed when Eduardo Ríos Sánchez learned to drive and obtained his driver's license. Eduardo was then the one who drove the car and given his many skills and gifts, who accompanied the hymns and songs with his guitar and his harmonious voice.

Eduardo Ríos was a good companion in many of the places where I established a missionary activity. I believe that missionary work is one of his gifts. I was mortified with him because of his traditional "absent-mindedness". He got lost in Pesquería, which at the time was a small town of no more than a hundred homes, and he confused the way back from that town to Ciego de Ávila and took the road to the north that leads to the central Primero de Enero, instead of to the south, which leads to the Central Highway. These "entertainments" bothered me, I scolded him, but he never was insulted or got upset with me, he never gave me an inappropriate response. His work in Chambas when I couldn't go was serious and responsible, and the congregation appreciated him. Unfortunately, like Demas in his relationship with Saint Paul, 2 Timothy 4:10, he abandoned us.

The current pastor of Emmanuel, Eduardo González Hernández, was my mission companion in Corojo. There we went to preach on Saturday afternoons when Bolivia and Chambas already had resident workers.

Traveling to Corojo without your own transportation was almost impossible, so the fact that Eduardito had a motorcycle made the transfer easier. Working as a driver, he learned missionary work and gained experience in pastoral care for a small universe of people. I will never be able to forget the afternoon when we were surprised by a tremendous downpour almost as we exited to the Central Highway. Eduardo asked me, "What do we do? Do I continue, or do I try to take shelter somewhere?" I chose to continue. Then, many people criticized me for that decision. We arrived home so wet that we could be squeezed but happy to have done our duty.

Another of the young people from our church who knew how to grow in missionary tasks was Abel Cotelo Pardo, who, every Tuesday night, accompanied me to services in the Canaleta neighborhood, southwest of Ciego de Ávila. Little by little, he grew in that work and was left alone in it until he entered the Evangelical Seminary of Theology in Matanzas. Before, during and after his studies in Matanzas, Abelito also collaborated with the work in the mission that we had established in the city of Morón. The services were held there in the temple of the Episcopal Church. The then bishop of that church, Miguel E. Tamayo Zaldívar, who was my personal friend, had agreed to it. Every Friday, with Ormara, Eduardo Ríos, or Abelito, we went to the celebration we held in that city. Morón was for Abelito, after his graduation from the Seminary, a magnificent school in his training as a pastor, which he has been performing with such quality in the United Church of the United States after he traveled to that country to join his family, resident in the northern nation.

Illobis González, the only girl from Emmanuel who stood out in missionary tasks after her graduation from the Evangelical Seminary of Los Pinos Nuevos and her return to this province, she replaced Abelito in caring for the mission of Morón. For more than a year, she fought to maintain that missionary work, which, very unfortunately, for various reasons, did not continue, and even when we later tried to revive it, it was not possible. Perhaps, as Ormara's grandmother once told me, "Morón is very hard on the Gospel." She herself, when she came in 1916 from Santa Isabel de las Lajas to reside in this province, established her domicile in that town with her three little daughters and her husband. A few months after residing in

Morón she opened a Sunday Bible School in her house, of which she said she had achieved very little, but she sowed the seed, and the growth is given by the Lord.

Rafael Almeida Valdés was another young man from Emmanuel who began his work as a spiritual guide, collaborating with me in missionary work. With him, I went more than once to Guasimales, Chambas, Bolivia and other places, but where his work was most relevant was in Colorado. Rafael had serious difficulties relating to his family, he practically had nowhere to live, and we already had the property that the Gethsemane Baptist Church in that town has today. Not without fear, I offered him to reside in that home. With this action, we solved his problem and managed to take care of the property. Little by little he took on the missionary work that I helped support. During the time that Rafael studied at the Evangelical Theology Seminary in Matanzas, he maintained the missionary work of that congregation, to which he returned upon completing his studies.

The fact of having planted missionary work in various places in the Baraguá municipality encouraged the desire to have a congregation in the capital of the municipality, that is, in Gaspar. At that time, the Corojo mission was pastorally guided by a young man named Ángel Luis Bernal, whom we met when he was working with another denomination in which, as he said, "they exploited him." One day, he came to my office crying because of the mistreatment of which he was a victim: more than preaching or educating in the faith, he had to run errands at the pastor's house, wash the car, and other tasks of that nature.

I was saddened by his situation and allowed him to begin to demonstrate his vocation by working in the Corojo mission, which was very distant from us. He didn't do his job badly. With the purpose of beginning missionary work in Gaspar, we illegally purchased a property. At that time, it was punishable to buy a home and even more so to dedicate it to evangelical worship, but we did it knowing what this could entail. In the end, I told myself, "Unfortunately, in our country, there is no law that regulates the life of religious institutions." The property was magnificent, located in a central location, with a good patio and a hall that, converted into a temple, admitted more than sixty people. We furnished the place: we got a Cuban flag, a new pulpit, benches, and a small table for communion. It was a welcoming temple, but not four months passed before a housing inspector summoned us to his office to give us the news of the eviction. The property was taken from us with all its furniture. My protest was worthless.

I managed to arrange an interview with the first secretary of the Municipal Committee of the Communist Party in Baraguá, who showed no signs of understanding. I demanded the return of the illegally seized furniture. I was promised its return, and I am still waiting for it. At that meeting, the leader told me that the confiscation of the property would make it possible to convert that central corner into a community benefit institution. Fifteen years later, the site has become a public dump. A few months later, Caridad Diego Bello, director of the Office of Attention to Religious Affairs of the Central Committee of the Party, visited the province and met with pastors and leaders of churches of Ciego de Ávila. I participated, and after the meeting, she wanted to talk to me. Friendly, she told me, "We were very surprised that you were capable of an illegality like the one you committed in Gaspar." I responded with the tone that I have sometimes regretted using, "I am not sorry for what I did. If I must commit something similar again, I would do it to fulfill the call to which God has called me". The day we have a law that regulates the activity of churches, then, and not now, I will follow it. We were never able to establish missionary work in Gaspar again.

It was inconceivable to me that I would be repressed in this way for an illegality when in the municipality itself, in a town called La Clementina, a "pastor," without any denominational connection, had built a temple on land owned by the state farm, with "resolved" materials outside the law. The end of that citizen was pitiful, as he concluded his work as a pseudo-pastor imprisoned for the corruption of minors. But he was not sanctioned for illegally building a masonry temple in La Clementina without denominational ties. Paradoxes of life. I have said on more than one occasion that this sad and painful situation was, for me, like a second call to the UMAP.

There were eighteen places where we established missionary work in the province of Ciego de Ávila between 1992 and 2001. Six churches emerged from that work: La Vid Verdadera, in Corojo; Gethsemane, in Colorado; Koinonia, in Pesquería; Gibeón, in La Ilusión; Bethany, in Chambas; and Canaan, in Bolivia. They all managed to acquire their own place for their activities, and in less than ten years, they also had a permanent worker for pastoral work.

Living According to the Circumstances

The Fraternity Of Baptists Churches Of Cuba (FIBAC)

In the years following January 1, 1959, enormous antagonisms arose in the Cuban Churches. On the one hand, a growing emigration of pastors and leaders to the United States, who thus renounced the vocational call to work for the evangelization of our people or to build the Kingdom of God in the midst of a changing society. On the other hand, a group of Christians of all confessions who found in the political changes that were taking place signs of the Kingdom of God. The former branded the latter as collaborators of the Revolution, or more, as communists and, even worse, as infiltrators in the Churches.

Little by little, the gap between them deepened, and the Churches suffered the departure of some towards other latitudes and of others towards partisan militancy and the abandonment of their ecclesial commitment. A third group was a victim of incomprehension and rejection by the Churches. Thus, small groups of Christians emerged who attempted a commitment from the Church with an "option for the poor." There was no doubt that the theological airs of the South reached us with the Latin American Liberation Theology.

In Cuba, the prophetic voice of some Cuban theologians was raised. Sergio Arce taught us with his little book *The Testimony of the Church in a Socialist Society*, while in the

Baptist tradition, Pastor Francisco Rodés left us in writing his *Validity of the message of Christ for our action*, which was first published in 1971.

Baptists from the three conventions organized a movement called the Baptist Student Worker Coordination of Cuba (COEBAC), and with its transformative and radical imprint, some churches assumed a clear, diaphanous, and sincere commitment to the social changes that challenged the Church from society.

In Havana, the Ebenezer Baptist Church of Marianao, and the El Jordán Church of the Mañana neighborhood were at the forefront of that position, while in Matanzas, that place was occupied by the First Baptist Church. In Santiago de Cuba, Bayamo, Camagüey, and Ciego de Ávila, to name a few places, members of the Churches tried to join their congregations in more radical positions and leave aside a dichotomous life in which they adopted an attitude committed to work and its institutions on weekdays and on Sundays they sought to "separate themselves from the world" in a trans mundane and sometimes pharisaical escapism.

Obviously, as the days went by, the confrontation took on more problematic nuances, and the pastors of the three aforementioned churches were separated by the ruling leadership of the Baptist Convention of Western Cuba. The churches, using their powers and respecting the Baptist principle of local church autonomy, supported their pastors and refused to accept a dismissal that did not come from the congregation. The result was that, in a frank attitude of disrespect, the conventional structure separated the three churches from its Convention.

Meanwhile, in other parts of the country, those who supported an option committed to an "effective testimony in today's Cuba and the contemporary world" were separated from their conventional and/or local positions and were subsequently expelled from the membership of the churches.

For a few months, pastors Raúl Suárez Ramos, Adalberto Cuéllar Martínez, and Francisco Rodés González, from the three western churches mentioned above, tried, with the support of their congregations, to return to the Convention, without positive results.

For its part, in the United States, the Southern Baptist Convention, representative of the most formal and profound Baptist conservatism and with an ultra-conservative theology, received serious criticism of its positions from within its structures. It was not long before honest and well-intentioned leaders of the largest Baptist structure in the United States lost prestige and capacity with their departure, some by their own decision, others by dishonorable expulsion, and other Baptist entities with a position much more coincident with the American moment were created.

One of those groups was the Alliance of Baptists of North America, created in 1987. One of its most significant founders, the Reverend Allan Neilly, met in July 1989 with Pastor Francisco Rodés and me at the home of the Reverend Roger Crook in Cary, North Carolina, where we both lived for three months to take an English language course at the Wake Technological School. From that conversation arose the idea that the three separate congregations of the Baptist Convention of Western Cuba and others that joined them or were created in the country could become another Baptist association. Due to the extensive theological, biblical, and ecclesiological coincidence between both entities, the Alliance of Baptists of North America would be fully willing to contribute to its establishment and development.

Upon his return to the country, the Reverend Francisco Rodés convinced two fellow ministers separated from the Western Convention and others of the alternative, it was possible to found their own Baptist structure.

On September 8, 1989, in a liturgical celebration held in the Ebenezer Baptist Church of Marianao, the Fraternity of Baptist Churches of Cuba was born.

The three founding churches were soon joined by the William Carey Baptist Church of El Vedado. Its pastor, Juan F. Naranjo, had protested the attitude assumed against his colleagues in the ministry, but instead of being listened to in a constructive spirit, he was rejected and found no alternative but to take the step forward and join the nascent denomination. Something similar, but due to different circumstances, happened with the pastors Lázaro Cuesta, from Yaguajay; Miguel Entenza, from Sancti Spíritus; and José Ferrer, from Guara. The Baptist church of Luyanó, with its pastor José López Martínez, joined the project without renouncing its affiliation to the Western Convention (it has been the only case in the history of Baptists in Cuba in which a congregation has had dual affiliation).

Shortly after, the Emmanuel Baptist Church was established in San José de las Lajas, which, under the leadership of Manuel Delgado, was the first congregation formed under the imprint of the FIBAC. This was later joined by the Kayros Baptist Church of Bayamo, under the spiritual guidance of three lay leaders: Elia Fonseca Ramírez, Perla Aguilera Ross, and Álvaro Pérez Poveda.

Over time, FIBAC added churches: in Ciego de Ávila, Emmanuel; in Holguín, Mount of Olives; in Piedrecitas, Camagüey, Clara Rodés in Memoriam; in Camagüey, Ebenezer, and others until reaching a number very close to fifty congregations.

In its beginnings, under the guidance of the founding generation, the theological, social, and ecclesiological thinking of the FIBAC was completely coincident with the position of the

Baptists at the time of the Radical Reformation. Their congregations, some very small in number, made themselves felt in their cities and stood out for being made up of men and women who lived their faith in the midst of the aspirations and attitudes of their present.

The second FIBAC assembly, also held at the Ebenezer church, was attended by three people from what would later become the Emmanuel Baptist Church of Ciego de Ávila. Two of them did not feel comfortable in that assembly in which attitudes and methods copied from the Western Convention were still perceived, but even so, as it was a possible alternative, our church agreed, in a meeting held on November 13, 1994, to apply to FIBAC for admission as a member.

For two years I was secretary of missions of the Fraternity. I felt very good about accomplishing this task, even though the missionary spirit that has characterized Baptists through the centuries was not evident in the majority of the leaders and churches that made up FIBAC. In that task, I had replaced the Reverend Remberto Ortiz from the church in the Arrechabaleta neighborhood, in Matanzas. Unfortunately, I had serious confrontations with this brother, who apparently felt diminished by my actions, a reason that led me to leave that responsibility after two years. I made that decision against the grain of my missionary call, especially because I did not see in the board of directors at that time any closeness to the position that had led me to the confrontation with Pastor Ortiz.

Our church, self-supporting since its inception, has fully exercised its right to congregational government by rejecting agreements not endorsed by the local church. Following Baptist tradition, a pastor who was ordained two years later without the Fraternity's support was chosen and even without the Fratrnity's participation, despite having been invited.

Perhaps due to the entry of people not related to Baptist tradition and principles, the FIBAC was changing the points of view that led to its foundation and losing the focus of a radical theology inserted in the aspirations and hopes of the people. To this was added an ecclesiology in which, as in the historical Cuban Baptist structures, the leaders were the highest authority, the ones that decided on the aspirations and projects of the congregations.

Another of the evils that afflict the structure is the isolation in which the churches located at "the east of Eden" or at "the east of Paradise" feel, that is, outside the territory of Havana and Matanzas. This is evidenced, among many other things, by the reality that to occupy certain management positions, one must reside in "paradisiacal" territory. There are few leaders outside of it who have reached leadership positions in the FIBAC. Many churches in the central and eastern parts of the country feel isolated and complain about not having the warmth of the structures that other congregations enjoy.

That patriotic, transformative, renewing, and radical fervor of the beginning faded away, and at the time of writing these lines, I consider that there is not much left of the social, political, theological, and ecclesiological impact of the nascent denomination. However, I think it is important to highlight that young leaders of the Fraternity strive to banish the negative signs that paralyze their actions among us. Proof of this is that the FIBAC achieved its inclusion in the Registry of Associations, acquired the status of a member church in the Council of Churches, and has been able to add four professors to the Evangelical Seminary in Matanzas, where almost all the denomination's workers study. In addition, the possibility of becoming part of the Board of Directors of that theological institution is being analyzed.

As in any human institution, at FIBAC, negative genes intersect with positive ones. I think it is up to the new generation of pastors and leaders, and especially the new congregations that have emerged, to return to the genesis of a denomination that marked in our country, within the evangelical world in general and the Baptist world in particular, a new sign of faith and commitment.

Living According to the Circumstances

The Pastoral Care Of People With Disabilities

I lived the experience of having a blind father who, with his patience and love, helped his brothers, cousins, and other relatives to face the visual disability that affected them. Seeing the zeal he showed during the Literacy Campaign in 1961 teaching them to read and write in the Braille System to several people. Also, witnessing his interest in recognizing people with disabilities in general and those lacking the sense of sight, in particular, formed me since my adolescence in the effort to make a more appropriate form possible to treat them.

I grew up in the First Baptist Church of Camagüey. I remember that as a child, I always went to Sunday Bible School with my maternal grandmother, América Pérez Guzmán. When I left the house every Sunday, my grandmother gave me two coins, one for the offering and the other to give to "blind Rogelio," as she called a blind brother who never missed a Sunday morning at our church. Rogelio was one of the first to arrive and occupied his seat in the place where the senior class met, called Matías San José in memory of a hardworking layman from that congregation and father of a large family of active members of the church.

At the end of Sunday School, Rogelio went out with his red and white wooden cane to the door of the temple, where many of the attendees gave him coins that served as financial support. For me, it was an almost liturgical act to give Rogelio the coin that my grandmother gave me.

When I grew up and went to Sunday School alone, my grandmother never stopped giving me the two coins that she had instituted when I was a child. She only stopped doing it in 1960, when I began to support myself financially by having begun my working life. What I learned took effect and the coins I used in both tasks were now part of my own income.

One day in mid-1962, when I was teaching as a Sunday School teacher, I was surprised not to see Brother Rogelio. It was the first time in my life that I did not see him in the temple on a Sunday morning. After the Sunday Bible School was over, I hurriedly went to the superintendent of the same, Brother Julio Jiménez Pérez, and asked him, "I was surprised not to see Brother Rogelio in the temple today, do you know anything about it?" Embarassed, he replied, "How could I forget to announce to the church that Brother Rogelio passed away on Thursday?"

That church, to which I owe so much, had not learned to treat Rogelio with the spirit of inclusion that emerges from the Scriptures: we had only dealt with his situation in a welfare-oriented manner. In my long ecclesial experience, I have not found, at least until now, a better congregation than that of the First Baptist Church of Camagüey. I have not witnessed the missionary and evangelistic zeal, the good stewardship, the fraternity, and the Christian fellowship that we had in it, not even in the churches of which I later became pastor. However, it did nothing to properly include Rogelio in the fold. I don't think it was a lack of love. I think it was just a lack of preparation to play the role that, as a community of faith, it had to assume.

When, at the end of 1989, I almost completely lost my sense of sight, I thought about the need to encourage in the Cuban Churches an adequate policy of pastoral care and inclusion of people with disabilities. My father's attitude, on the one hand, and the memory of the abandonment to which we subjected Brother Rogelio, on the other, were motivations to dream, think, and pray that the churches in Cuba would be able to assume their evangelical role in the appropriate treatment of the issue of disability.

This is how, in May 1990, thanks to the help of Reverend Pedro Mayor, a Methodist pastor who was responsible for coordinating the Commission of Secular Activities of the Council of Churches of Cuba, I obtained resources to hold the First Meeting of the Blind of the Cuban Churches. In the facilities of the Methodist Church of K and 25 of El Vedado, in Havana, we managed to bring together twenty-four blind and low-vision people from various places in the country – Holguín, Santa Clara, Santo Domingo, Cotorro, Jagüey Grande, Havana and Ciego de Ávila – which were part of Baptist, Methodist,

Pentecostal and Quaker churches. The activity was a suitable incentive to think big. Similar events were held at the same location in 1991 and 1992.

At the first of the Board of Directors' Meetings of the Council of Churches in 1992, I presented a motion requesting the creation of a department or commission for differently qualified people. The motion did not enthuse Reverend Sergio Arce, who represented the Presbyterian Church on the Board at the time, nor Joel Ajo, who was participating on behalf of the Methodist Church. Both opposed my proposal, arguing strongly that it would be a form of exclusion that would go against the spirit of inclusion and unity of the Council.

Both Dr. Arce and Reverend Ajo were my friends, people who had my deep affection. From the first, I had learned most of the theology that I support, and the second had been my partner in struggle in the ecumenical bustle of the previous two decades. I talked with them at length, so much so that I managed to change their points of view. At the second Board of Directors, held in November of the same year, they were, together with me, promoters of the creation in the Council of a department called Coordination for the Disabled, of which I was appointed its Coordinator.

As a first task, we did research on the number of people with disabilities who made up Cuban Churches. Even though this investigation was not as exhaustive as I had intended, it yielded a certain amount of information that showed us that they were totally turning their back on pastoral work with that universe of people.

We only found twenty-six blind people as active members of the evangelical and Protestant churches in the country. The number of deaf people was much smaller, four. We were not able to find out how many people with physical-motor limitations made up the membership of the Churches. It was surprising to me to discover that in the Pentecostal Christian Church of Artemisia, a woman who used a wheelchair, Cristina Rodríguez, served as pastor. The commendable work of this sister was a cause for admiration, given the religious fervor characteristic of Pentecostalism. Cristina vibrated with excitement at each liturgical celebration, and her chair practically jumped with the joy that she brought to each meeting of her church.

Another person who motivated us in this task was pastor Rita Morris – married to pastor Raymundo García Franco, who pastored the Presbyterian Church of Cárdenas – who was losing her hearing ability little by little. Rita was not intimidated by her situation, and she found in the life of her church first, and then the Christian Center of Reflection and Dialogue, new forms of service and Christian commitment. Many of us have enjoyed Sister Rita Morris's compilations of texts that enrich the spirituality of the churches and greatly help to complete Christian worship in our services and public gatherings.

Living According to the Circumstances

Initially, our work focused on pastoral care for people with visual disabilities. For us, the presence at one of our meetings of the Cuban troubadour José Tejedor, who had become blind months before and participated in the life of the Baptist Church of La Víbora, was an exciting incentive. Also relevant was, in another of the first meetings, the attendance of Mr. José Monteagudo, then vice president of the National Association of the Blind (ANCI) and later president of the Latin American Union of the Blind (ULAC), who was accompanied by Mr. Ilse Bulit, whom the Cuban people knew from the pages of the popular *Bohemia* magazine. Ilse was in charge of the Cultural Section in that publication. She had lost her sense of sight a few months before and was experiencing the existential crisis that such a situation causes in almost all of us who go through this experience. She had no religious culture, and the concept of faith in God was far from her life project. Our event, without intending to be an evangelistic activity, reached the mind and heart of Ilse, who, from then on, chose Jesus Christ as the motive for her actions. Years later, when Habana Radio, the station of the Havana Historian's Office, was inaugurated, Ilse Bulit joined the station and has had a laudable role there.

Before the celebration of the fourth meeting of the blind men and women of the Cuban Churches, the first of many held in the National Camp of the Presbyterian Church (CANIP) in Santa

Clara, the work was structured, and the objectives that we would assume were made known:

- Provide a space for the biblical-theological training of people with disabilities in accordance with their characteristics and needs.
- Train pastors and church leaders in appropriate care for people with disabilities.
- Raise awareness in local churches about the real possibilities of realization in the Work of this group of brothers and sisters, as well as combat feelings of paternalism, pity and manipulation, promoting a real inclusion of them in local communities.
- Work closely with theological institutions to incorporate the topic of disability into their curriculum.
- Serve as bridges to create links of cooperation with associations of people with disabilities in the country and, when necessary, with other agencies abroad in order to obtain resources for the full inclusion of people with disabilities.
- Contribute to the existing practice in the country of including people with disabilities in the full life of society, with the church also being a factor of rehabilitation and inclusion.

From that moment on, a broad plan of activities began to be developed that, with the intention of fulfilling the proposed objectives, has sought to encompass all the Churches in the country, regardless of their respective doctrinal emphases, traditions, and customs. From the very beginning, no Christian confession was excluded from the Pastoral work, so it was not at all strange that Roman Catholics worshiped alongside Seventh-day Adventists or Episcopalians alongside Pentecostals.

A special emphasis was on working with people who are deafblind. On the occasion of a tour across the eastern provinces with the pastor Xiomara Arenas, then director of the Women's Department of the Council, and Ormara, who served as director of the Department of Renewal of the Church, we visited, at the suggestion of the Reverend Gilberto Prieto, the Babiney Baptist Church, in the municipality of Cauto Cristo, Granma. The Reverend Carlos Alamino pastored that congregation since his graduation from the Baptist Seminary of Eastern Cuba. Reverend Alamino told us about the sadness that overwhelmed him at the beginning of his activity in Babiney when he was not able to communicate with the group of deafblind people in the town, some of whom were members of the Figueredo family, which for many years had been part of that community of faith. He then told us that even unscrupulous people mocked them and forced them to do indecorous and unpleasant acts. The young pastor decided to do something to change the situation. His efforts to educate those who harassed people with deafblindness were not very successful, so he considered that the most appropriate thing was to get deafblind people to know the Lord Jesus Christ.

Reverend Alamino managed to create his own method of communication and a Sunday School class – as far as I know, the only one in a Baptist church in Latin America and perhaps in the entire world – that would serve to bring to the feet of the Lord people deprived of both senses. Alamino's project was successful and thirteen local deafblind people have given public testimony of their faith in baptism. The visit to Babiney's church had a positive impact on all of us, and I especially felt challenged to increase my knowledge on the subject and incorporate work with this universe of people into Pastoral Care.

Years later, in 2011, we managed to get the Evangelical Theology Seminary (SET) to offer a distance learning course aimed at training guides-interpreters for deafblind people in the Cuban Churches. The course was the result of Sergio Troyano Botello's graduation thesis, titled "A pastoral ministry that contributes to the improvement of care for people with deafblindness in the Babiney Baptist Church," which recommended the implementation of that course to the SET.

Every year since 1998, a meeting of people with deafblindness from Cuban churches has been held at the facilities of the Los Amigos Church in Gibara, attended by members of five congregations, all located in the provinces of

Holguín, Granma, and Santiago de Cuba. It is worth recognizing that there are currently other congregations in the country, outside of the aforementioned provinces, where pastoral care for these people is carried out.

In January 2011, the Pastoral Ministry organized and carried out the First National Forum on Deaf-Blindness at the SET facilities. We received help from the Chair of Disability Studies of the Faculty of Psychology of the University of Havana, of which I was a part, and we had the presence of representatives from the Directorate of Special Schools of the Ministry of Education, the Ministry of Culture, the Ministry of Public Health, the Ministry of Labor, the National Institute of Sports, Physical Education and Recreation, as well as the National Association of the Blind, the National Association of the Deaf and churches interested in the subject. The idea was to join forces in more comprehensive training for the benefit of people with deafblindness in our country. It was a very relevant activity. Rarely in Cuban history has the Church taken initiatives that combine training, educational, cultural, political, and economic efforts, as that forum turned out to be.

Although the intentions of the Pastoral Ministry have always been to work with all types of disabilities, work with deaf people was practically non-existent. Perhaps, the difficulties of communication between blind and deaf people limited, at least in the initial stages of the work, what we could do with them. But

Living According to the Circumstances

in June 1994, Brother Ernesto Clark, son of an American woman who had worked as a missionary and teacher at the Los Pinos Nuevos Evangelical Seminary in Oliver, Placetas, arrived at the offices of the Council of Churches. Because he spent part of his childhood in Cuba, he felt special closeness to the Cubans. Brother Clark had dedicated his time to ministry with deaf people and had accomplished excellent work in Mexico, and especially in Jamaica. In the latter country he had founded and supported a school for deaf people with the resources of his mission agency.

Clark showed great missionary zeal. At the invitation of the then Executive Secretary of the Council, Reverend Otoniel Bermúdez, I interviewed him, and he expressed his deep interest in ministry with deaf people. Unaware, as Brother Clark was then of the Cuban reality, he proposed to us the possibility of founding and supporting schools in Cuba for the education of deaf people in which, in addition, we would present to them the message of salvation in Jesus Christ. It was quite difficult for me to convince him that it was not necessary to create schools for the education of deaf people on Cuban soil. However, I supported his intention to work, through Pastoral Care, in the Christian education of deaf people residing in the country.

Months later, he returned to the country to continue the conversations that had begun. It was on that occasion, taking advantage of the chance presence of Reverend Gilberto Prieto at the headquarters of the Council of Churches of Cuba, that I invited him to participate in the meeting with the visitor from the United States, the executive secretary of the Council, and myself.

Pastor Prieto, who was then serving at the First Baptist Church of Guantánamo, had had recent experiences with deaf people. A couple with that disability had attended his congregation and had learned about the message of salvation of Jesus Christ, to which it had joined. Undoubtedly, he was a key person for that type of work. We agreed, then, to begin working with deaf people within the framework of the Pastoral Ministry and I asked Reverend Prieto for his collaboration.

In December of that same year, we realized that Cuban sign language did not have any signs to communicate the truths of the Christian faith. Realizing that deaf people had no way to "hear" and "say" words like God, Jesus Christ, salvation, abundant life, Kingdom of God, Bible, cross, resurrection, etc., we called a meeting of deaf people, interpreters, biblical scholars and pastors with experience to create signs in the Cuban language for the deaf that would express those terms of the Christian faith. It was hard work, carried out in the facilities of the First Baptist Church of Guantánamo. In the end, more than one hundred words from religious language were incorporated into Cuban sign language.

Living According to the Circumstances

This task was followed by an even more complicated one: getting the National Association of the Deaf (ANSOC) and the Ministry of Education to agree to include the new terms in the Cuban Sign Language dictionary. It was a battle of months that was finally crowned with the approval of the ANSOC specialists. It was necessary to modify some signs, change others, work "side by side" with the Association, but in the end, we managed to ensure that the deaf people of Cuba could learn about the values of Christianity in their own language.

The work with deaf people was intensified with the collaboration of Brother Clark, given his experience and cooperation. It became necessary to organize a Cuban work team with deaf people – a suggestion that we accepted from Brother Clark – which we baptized with the name of Deaf Ears, Hearing Hearts (OSCO), and which was made up of the Reverend Gilberto Prieto as coordinator, the Reverend Gisela Pérez Muñiz as secretary and treasurer, Reverend Elmer Lavastida Alfonso and Sister Nérida Rodés as members. I was named team manager. Twice a year, we met with Brother Clark to evaluate the work, analyze new endeavors, and rejoice in the growth throughout the country of pastoral and evangelistic work with the Cuban deaf community. OSCO was a kind of subprogram of the Pastoral Care of People with Disabilities specialized in working with deaf and hard of hearing people, in which, as in all Pastoral activities, people and Churches who were members or not of the Council participated.

The activity, which was carried out with unity and Christian fraternity, was clouded when, in one of the team meetings, Reverend Prieto announced that OSCO had been assumed as a ministry affiliated with the Baptist Convention of Eastern Cuba. He said that, when making that decision, it had been difficult for them to accept that a pastor from a church not affiliated with the Convention be their director, but that after several analyses and discussions, it was agreed to receive OSCO, including me as their director. I felt upset because I had not been consulted beforehand, and what had been discussed in the group until then was in the initial plans: the work with the deaf would be endorsed by the Pastoral Care of Personnel with Disabilities and integrated into it, which, as it was a program of the Church Council, it did not require any other structure to give it official support.

OSCO's work continued with the growth in the number of deaf people in the churches, the formation of new interpreters, and biblical and theological training plans for deaf and hard-of-hearing people. I never managed to be a teacher of these courses, and neither was the Reverend Gisela Pérez, but we both participated in the meetings of deaf people, interpreters, and pastors that took place every two years at the Canaan camp of the Methodist Church.

Living According to the Circumstances

I was forced to leave my responsibility at OSCO. I understood that my presence, more than an effective help, constituted a brake on the programs that were developed, which were not always methodologically and theologically consistent with my points of view. But despite these discrepancies, the Lord, in his mercy, allowed the relations of fraternity between those of us who, in one way or another, were part of OSCO and the Pastoral Care of People with Disabilities to not be affected. This attitude on both sides allowed them to develop joint work. Perhaps the most important was the translation into Cuban sign language for the deaf of texts from the Second Testament.

A team was created to translate Bible texts for deaf Cubans, which was made up of six deaf people, two interpreters, and a theological and methodological advisor. These represented the Deaf Ears, Hearing Hearts ministry, the Free of Silence ministry, and deaf people of the Catholic Church, as well as qualified personnel from the Pastoral Care of People with Disabilities of the Council of Churches of Cuba. The advice of Dr. Elsa Tamez from the United Bible Societies was vital in the formation of the team. Dr. Tamez's interest and her experience in translating biblical texts in Costa Rica motivated the United Bible Societies to provide financial support to the activity. It is worth noting that missionary Paola Inocente, from the *Latina Link* Ministry, also shared with the team her experience in this type of work, acquired in Colombia and Peru.

Living According to the Circumstances

The work of the CIC Biblical Commission was very relevant. Due to the content of the translation team's work, it logically had to be assigned to that program of the Council of Churches of Cuba. The Reverend Alain Montano, in his capacity as executive secretary of the Biblical Commission, assumed his responsibility until the culmination of the first four stories carried out and presented to the deaf community on December 3, 2012, in the Episcopal Church of Cienfuegos first, and later in many other places in the country. Unfortunately, the Pastoral Care of People with Disabilities did not continue the work begun to translate biblical texts into Cuban sign language. A team made up of two deaf people, one of them Alejandro Torres, who serves as its director, and an interpreter, based in the SET – which is obviously of capital importance – it is subordinated to the Biblical Commission. Unfortunately, the team has gradually been ignoring and disregarding our contribution and our history.

A very significant place in the activity of the Pastoral Care of People with Disabilities was played by the Reverend Antonio Padilla. This unforgettable brother was part of the Assembly of Brothers, in Spain, a name that in Cuba is officially called Evangelical Rooms. Padilla, a prosperous businessman, lost his sight in a domestic accident, which was a blow from which he believed he would never recover. However, his faith in Christ and the help of the Brethren Assemblies in Spain and other places in Europe encouraged him to use his gifts in many ways.

Living According to the Circumstances

One of them was the creation of a ministry for blind and low-vision people in Spain and Latin America called Nueva Luz. We established relations with that organization, and since then, we have had the presence of Reverend Padilla. First, in almost all of the Christian Blind Meetings and then National Committees for People with Disabilities of the Cuban Churches. His great biblical ability and his eloquent way of teaching captivated the sisters and brothers who attended our activities. With him, we visited various cities throughout the island, helping churches understand the issue of disability so that they could include it in their areas of work. In relationships with Nueva Luz, we have achieved wide support. Their books, in Braille format and on cassettes, then on discs, and his periodical publications are very well received. It is also worth highlighting the financial support they have given us.

Thanks to Nueva Luz, we managed, between 2012 and 2014, to donate a copy of the Bible in Braille system to all the provincial public libraries, to seven municipal ones, to the Cultural Recreational Center of the ANCI, to the libraries of the Adventist Seminary and the Evangelical Seminary of Theology and the National Library. In each of these places, programs were held with the presence of blind and low-vision people from the localities where these institutions were located, in which not only the Holy Scriptures were donated, but extensive information about the sacred text of Christianity was shared.

Worth mentioning has been the work we have done together with the Ministry of Joni and Friends and the Cuban Association of People with Physical-Motor Limitations (ACLIFIM) in the distribution of wheelchairs and Bibles to people who need them. I dedicate an entire chapter to this important and necessary work.

Thanks to the initiative of Dr. María Teresa García Eligio de la Puente, dean of the Faculty of Psychology at the University of Havana, in February 2004, the Chair of Disability Studies was created at that center of higher education, of which was invited to take part in the Pastoral Care of People with Disabilities. I was involved, representing it, throughout the Chair's program. It is worth highlighting the respect and sympathies that both Dr. García and Mr. Blas Eduardo Mora Maestre, secretary of the Chair, showed towards the work that we carried out from the Council of Churches of Cuba. Our participation served, among many other things, to establish magnificent working relationships with the members, among them Yusimí Campos, who, in her capacity as director of the Department of Security and Social Assistance of the Ministry of Labor, was an integral part of the aforementioned university. These relationships were very useful when the Pastoral Ministry required, for its project Full Life for Social Inclusion in Equal Rights and Opportunities of People with Disabilities, to link up with the Ministry of Labor and Social Security. The course offered at the Chair's headquarters, located in the Faculty of Psychology, to thirty-five collaborators of people with disabilities from different regions of the country and churches was significant.

The Church World Service proposed that the Pastoral Ministry of People with Disabilities take over the coordination of the Action Church Together (ACT) Community of Practice on Disability. Thus, we are part of a network of organizations and institutions of people with disabilities and/or for people with disabilities on a global scale. After four years in that complex job, during a meeting held in Indonesia I requested to leave that responsibility in the hands of another person due to my limitations with the English language. ACT thanked us for the work done and spoke highly of the knowledge and experience learned from the work we did in Cuba.

The biblical, theological, and social improvement of people with disabilities in the Cuban Churches and the inclusion of the issue of disability in the theological institutions of the country have always been priorities of the Pastoral Ministry. In this sense, good relations were achieved with the Baptist Theological Seminary of Eastern Cuba in Santiago de Cuba and even better relations with the Evangelical Theological Seminary in the city of Matanzas. In the course concluded in 2002, graduate Yodalis Santiago was the first to present a thesis related to the topic of disability, which was very well received by the institution's faculty. Subsequently, Sergio Troyano presented his thesis on people with deafblindness. Years later, Sister Santiago submitted another thesis on the topic of disability to obtain her master's degree. However, the most relevant fact in relation to theological studies of people with disabilities in Cuba - without forgetting the young blind David Oliva, who in 1952 graduated from the Evangelical Seminary of Los Pinos Nuevos with a bachelor's degree in Theology - was the studies from Brother Rolando Verdecia Ávila. His degree in Theology and then in his relevant thesis entitled "Rereading 1st Corinthians 12:12-26 for a foundation of the inclusion paradigm from the perspective of people with disabilities". Not satisfied with these studies, Brother Verdecia prepared between 2015 and 2017 at the South American Seminary (Semisud) of the Church of God in Quito, Ecuador in cooperation with Lee University in Cleveland, to obtain his master's degree. At the time of writing these lines, he is pursuing doctoral studies in Theology at that institution.

Thanks to the enthusiastic and determined cooperation of Dr. Ester Bollag from the University of Hamburg in Germany, the Pastoral Ministry enrolled two students in the SET: José Julián Fontela, with low vision, and Yoelkis Morales, totally blind, to study with residence at the facility, a bachelor's degree in theological studies. At the same time, a group of seven young people with disabilities studied the high school distance learning course in Biblical and Theological Studies.

Living According to the Circumstances

For its part, the SET has included the topic of disability in its curriculum in various ways, especially in the preparation of graduates in Christian Education. It is important to add that the SET has as part of its annual programming a day dedicated to the issue of disability with the title Day of the Gifts of People with Disabilities.

In 2015, a project sponsored by the European Union (EU) and co-sponsored by *Christopher Blinder Mission* (CBM) was launched entitled "Full life for social inclusion in equal rights and opportunities for people with disabilities." The aim, among other things, was to promote with work ventures the social inclusion of people with disabilities in six municipalities of the country in the provinces of: Ciego de Ávila, Camagüey, Las Tunas, and Granma. The project managed to initiate relations between the Council of Churches of Cuba and the Ministry of Labor and Social Security, which had never been established before and which demonstrated the unity of criteria and interests of the Church in Cuba with a government entity. Also relevant was the holding of awareness sessions with the residents and decision-makers of the forty-eight popular councils of the municipalities involved in the project.

As a result of a planning and institutional renewal process of the Council of Churches, the Pastoral Care of People with Disabilities became part of its Diaconic Area. Together with Health and Community Life, Sustainable Development,

Emergency, and Churches Help Churches, and under the successful coordination of Dr. Elina Ceballos, our work had much more recognition and institutional support.

During the time –already long– in which the work of people with disabilities has existed in the CIC, we have been presided over by various personalities from the ecumenical life of the nation: Orestes González, Raúl Suárez, Odén Marichal, Reinerio Arce, Rhodes González, Marcial Miguel Hernández, Joel Ortega Dopico and Antonio Santana. None of them were oblivious to the work we did, but it was Brother Joel Ortega Dopico who felt our work was his own and has demonstrated with actions, his awareness of the work of the Pastoral Ministry. I cannot fail to express my gratitude to him here.

On February 12, 2019, the board of directors of the Council of Churches of Cuba received, through the national team of the Pastoral Care of People with Disabilities, the request for the release of the general coordinator of the program and the recommendation to appoint Master Rolando Verdecia Ávila to that position. There were almost twenty-nine years of beautiful work in which this program achieved significant impacts, such as:

- Of the seventy-eight interpreters for the deaf trained to work in churches, twelve have been employed by the National Association of the Deaf to serve as interpreters in secular life. Almost all of them have graduated in this discipline after our introductory course. Five of them have enrolled in the country's universities to continue studies in this specialty.

- From two people with disabilities linked full-time as "workers in the Lord's Vineyard" at the beginning of our work, today, thanks to the training provided, their number has increased to fifty-eight pastors, priests, and missionaries.
- None of the fifty-four evangelical or Protestant denominations in the country, nor the Catholic Church, have rejected collaboration with the program. Nine of them have requested advice for the implementation of their own programs on the subject. Since 2005, twenty-seven denominations have developed projects and/or programs with people with disabilities; none did so in 1990. The training of collaborators and the care and training of people with disabilities has not made the exception of any denomination or religious entity.
- The Chair of Disability Studies of the Faculty of Psychology of the University of Havana has organized events and activities in conjunction with the Program. The Program Coordinator is an advisor to the Chair. Other people linked to the Pastoral Ministry have participated in its events and activities. The Pastoral Ministry and the Chair have offered two distance learning

Special Psychology courses, from which fifty-five collaborators of people with disabilities have graduated.

- The United Bible Societies accepted criticism about the use of pejorative and obsolete terms related to the issue of disability in current translations of the Bible. They requested arguments in this regard, and their request was heeded. A critical presentation was submitted, analyzed, and discussed at the meeting of Bible translators held in Montevideo, Uruguay, in March 2008.
- Thanks to the publication of a Glossary of useful terms used in the promotion of a culture of disability in both ecclesiastical and social sectors, the use of appropriate terms is being achieved in the treatment of people with disabilities in churches, NGOs, government agencies, and mass media.
- The annual holding of an arts festival workshop with people with disabilities from the Cuban Churches and an annual musical composition contest has led to the promotion and dissemination of the artistic talent of ninety-one people with disabilities. The result of this work is the recording of the CD *Somos el Trío Emmanuel* by the musical group of the same name, made up of blind and low-vision people from the First Baptist Church of Guantánamo. This record production, which contains original pieces by the trio and stands out for the presence

of genres and rhythms typical of traditional Cuban music and typical of the region, has been disseminated and promoted both in our country and abroad, as a result of which The Trio Emmanuel has performed numerous times on national stages, as well as in the capital and the Andean region of Ecuador, and made a memorable presentation on the prestigious radio station HCJB La Voz de los Andes, in Quito.

- The holding of four national and territorial meetings of Christian women with disabilities, as well as two collective marriages of people with disabilities (forty-nine couples), has had a highly positive impact on the work with a gender focus carried out by the Pastoral Ministry. In these spaces, topics related to different manifestations of violence against women with disabilities and the prevention of sexually transmitted diseases, among others, have been addressed.
- In all our national meetings in 2009, we included the study and debate of the International Convention on the Rights of People with Disabilities, approved by the UN General Assembly, which has resulted in the awareness of people with disabilities in the Cuban Churches about their rights to participation and equal opportunities in all spaces of social life.

- To date, the Pastoral has published the following materials:
    i. Pastoral Book *Of The Other Heart*
    ii. Brochure *"How to be supportive of differently-abled people."*
    iii. Folding "Tips for good communication with blind people."
    iv. Folding "How to improve your communication with the deaf."
    v. Folding "Evangelistic tract for the deaf"
    vi. Foldable "God Speaks in Cuban Sign Language (John 3:16)" (first in the Bible *Verses in Cuban Sign Language series*)
    vii. Book *Women, Violence and Disability*
    viii. Brochure *"Are all families the same?"*

These publications constitute an unprecedented contribution both in the ecclesial and social spheres of our country, which have also had a great impact on other nations in Latin America, North America, and Europe.

Living According to the Circumstances

Joni And Friends - JAF

I learned of the existence of Joni Eareckson Tada from the Reverend José López, who was working at that time as coordinator of the Biblical Commission of the Council of Churches of Cuba. Pepe, as we usually call him, had been for many years the leader of the Baptist Convention of Western Cuba, in which he served as secretary during several school periods. I knew him from his presence at the assemblies of the Eastern Convention in Santiago de Cuba, which he attended every February, always accompanied by his noble and friendly wife, Ladinela Rubio. He was a pastor for many years in the Baptist Church of Luyanó, and even with his well-defined institutional commitment, he always maintained a relationship of brotherhood with those of us who participated in the COEBAC. When the Fraternity of Baptist Churches of Cuba was organized in September 1989, the congregation he pastored joined it as an observing church.

This brother traveled with Reverend Marcial Miguel Hernández to a Pan American Congress of Evangelism in Los Angeles, California, in 1988, and, as far as I have been able to know, they were the first Cubans who personally met Joni Eareckson Tada, of whose ministry and testimony there were already references in the country. The contact was informal, and the Cubans could only greet Sister Joni. Subsequently, twenty-eight Cuban evangelical leaders attended an Evangelistic

Congress of the Billy Graham Association in Amsterdam, Holland, in which Joni played a relevant role. Among them was Dr. Ondina Maristany, leader of the Baptist Convention of Eastern Cuba, who spoke to me with enthusiasm about Joni's work. Some of the Cuban assistants exchanged experiences with her and invited her to visit our country to learn about the work that the Council of Churches had been doing with people with disabilities. Upon his return, Reverend López told me that he felt very favorably impressed by Joni's testimony and the ministry she was developing in the United States.

A few months later, on one of my periodic work visits to the offices of the Council of Churches of Cuba, I found a brochure where the objectives and activities of the JAF Ministry were announced. The address of Agoura Hills, in California, appeared, where they would provide more information to those who requested it. Without thinking twice, I wrote directly to Sister Joni. It was the time when postal mail from Cuba to the United States took more than a month, and it was not certain that the letters would reach their destination. I never had a response to that letter in which I remember saying to Sister Joni, "I hope that one day you and I can meet there or here, where you will be very well received."

I don't know how they located me, but John Wern, then director of the **Wheels for the World** program from the Joni and Friends Ministry, scheduled me to meet him in May 1998 at the

Living According to the Circumstances

Marianao Methodist Church facilities. I arrived before Brother Wern, who arrived accompanied by several Americans. Wern looked nervous, as if scared. We stopped to talk on the side of the church's educational building while the companions took down boxes and packages. I think the conversation lasted about twenty minutes. The objective was to arrange an interview to let me know about the ministry he coordinated and the possibility of extending it to Cuba. We agreed to meet in Santiago de Cuba a year later. On the agreed date, I asked Reverend Elmer Lavastida to accompany me to the facilities of the Versailles Motel in the aforementioned city. Elmer would help me a lot in communication. His English language proficiency was essential to me.

Mr. Doug Mazza, president of the Joni and Friends Ministry, Pastor Gene Richardson, and John Wern as coordinator of the **Wheels for the World** program, participated in the event. They told of their international experience in the distribution of wheelchairs, which they collected through donations in the United States and then sent to federal prisons where prisoners, most sentenced to life in prison, repaired them and later packaged them to be sent to places as different as China, Ghana, Romania, Peru, El Salvador, Haiti, to mention some destinations. It seemed easy, but from my point of view, it became more complex when they explained to me that it was not just about donating wheelchairs but that with them would come a delegation of American physiatrists and mechanics to adjust the chairs to the reality of those who received them. They explained that these people would pay their own expenses and would take the workdays in Cuba from their vacations. Receiving a group of that nature would obviously require official procedures, visas, etc. I thought it would be impossible. What seemed even more difficult to me was that they told me that the delivery of wheelchairs and their adjustment should be followed by the delivery of a Bible to each of the people who received them, to whom the message of the abundant life of the Lord Jesus Christ should be presented.

We said goodbye after a long conversation in which they had introduced me to an activity that I believed would be of great blessing to those who lived with a disability that made them dependent on wheelchairs, which were then very deficient in our country. However, I did not consider the project feasible as they conceived it and had carried it out in several countries around the world. I discussed the situation with my brother and ministry partner, Lavastida. "Do you think it is possible that we can find a place for the distribution that is not a church facility, deliver a copy of the Bible there, and present the message?" And I added, "Elmer, that's impossible." With a feeling of hope, and as if to encourage me, he replied, "Hey, baseball players hit the ball as many times as they can to get a run."

Living According to the Circumstances

Reverend Lavastida's enthusiasm was contagious. A few days later, I requested an interview to discuss the issue at the Religious Affairs Office of the Party Central Committee. The official who assisted me after I explained the objectives and procedures of the new endeavor told me, "Noel, and who told you that this cannot be done in Cuba?" She limited herself to making some recommendations that seemed logical to me, "Never impose faith as a requirement for handing over wheelchairs. If someone does not want to receive the Bible, respect their discretion. The Cuban Association of People with Physical-Motor Limitations (ACLIFIM) is the organization that best knows who requires wheelchairs in the country. Therefore, this must be a coordinated project with them: do not turn the Church into a wheelchair distribution agency."

From that moment we began preparations for the first delivery of wheelchairs brought by JAF. To do this, we coordinated with ACLIFIM, which was the non-governmental organization in the country that knew where those who needed wheelchairs were. Added to this was that ACLIFIM itself offered its facilities at the 26 de Julio Training Center (CENCAP), located in El Cacahual, Havana, to make the first delivery.

From the beginning, the presentation of the Bible to the person who obtained the wheelchair, and the subsequent message was carried out by me until later, I shared that task with the Reverend Sergio Troyano and the Reverend Ramona

Matos. Later, Reverend Rafael Mullet replaced Reverend Troyano. Of the almost seven thousand people to date who have been the object of our work, only three have rejected the Bible that we offered them. Two were members of the Jehovah's Witnesses sect and politely stated that the translation we offered them was not "the true one." Obviously, they preferred the translation of The Watchtower. The other was a woman who identified herself as "daughter of the Devil and enemy of God."

In the work done person by person, we have been very blessed. Each individual receives from the team of pastors guidance, encouragement, pastoral accompaniment, brotherly love. Some make the option of faith in Jesus Christ, others have returned to the faith, some decide to reconcile with their churches, others ask interesting questions, but almost all of the beneficiaries show interest and gratitude.

The relations with ACLIFIM deserve a separate paragraph, which at first were simply diplomatic. The then president of the Association, Ida Hilda Escalona, always treated us courteously and accepted our collaboration, but she was not personally interested in the initiative. Relations changed drastically when Mabel Ballesteros assumed the presidency. Since then, and over the years, she has been a tireless fighter for the improvement of relations, not only with the Pastoral Care of People with Disabilities but with the Council of Churches of Cuba in general. Furthermore, she has created in her NGO an environment of camaraderie, fellowship, and human sensitivity that brings her closer, perhaps without even intending to, to the values of the Gospel. This relationship of unity and fraternity has not only been established with the national leadership of the Association, but in the provinces where the work has been carried out, we have enjoyed the same fraternity in the common effort to contribute to the well-being of the people who come looking for their wheelchair.

It is worth noting that the physiatrists and mechanics who travel from the United States twice a year to do this work are increasingly supportive, expressive, and friendly. Although at first there was a seemingly insurmountable distance and coldness in the vast majority of them, today, on the contrary, we maintain very pleasant relations, and the Cuban group integrates with them as a single work team.

Sister Bonnie Banker, who since March 2007 has coordinated the effort of the Dallas, Texas office of the JAF Ministry for work with Cuba, has been instrumental in the development of more fraternal relationships, deeper work, and adequate understanding of the Cuban situation that she strives to convey to foreign visitors.

Starting in 2011, JAF has added Family Retreats to its work on Cuban soil. Three of them, first in Ciego de Ávila and later in Santiago de Cuba, have brought together families of people with disabilities for four days so that they can enjoy vacation, prepare to face their realities, exchange experiences, and receive psychological guidance. The special thing about this effort is that each family has an accompanying missionary, who is responsible for the care and attention of the boy, girl, or adolescent in the family, thus giving the possibility for adults to participate in the program appropriately and all the time necessary. The retreats also allow church leaders to be trained in the culture of disability. However, the most significant aspect of our relations with Joni's ministry was her visit to our country. It was May 2003 when, amidst overflowing joy, Sister Joni Eareckson Tada landed at the Santiago de Cuba airport, the first stop on her short but unforgettable trip to Cuba. At the airport facility itself, Joni remembered the letter in which I had told her that one day we would meet. Incredibly, this became a reality at the Santiago airport.

With an attendance difficult to match, the Second Baptist Church of Santiago de Cuba opened its doors for the first of the three services in which the distinguished visitor would oversee exposing the message of the Word. Joni herself would later comment that she had rarely had the experience of having so many people with different disabilities in a service in which she was the preacher.

In the city of Havana, in addition to a fraternal lunch with leaders of the Council of Churches of Cuba and Cuban Churches, she preached at the Episcopal Cathedral of the Holy

Trinity and at the El Calvario Baptist Church. They were two unforgettable liturgical celebrations that sympathy, charisma, and mastery of the gift of words, together with extensive biblical knowledge, turned into spaces of blessing.

The liturgical celebration in the Baptist Church of Zulueta y Dragones constituted her farewell to Cuban soil. From that place, the distinguished visitor and her companions hurriedly left to board her flight back to the United States. But before her, the congregation, overflowing with joy and sympathy, gave her a farewell that was impossible to forget.

In February 2015, I met her again in California, where, accompanied by the Reverend Eduardo González, an indispensable organizer of all the logistics of wheelchair deliveries in Cuba, I participated in the *Global Access Conference*. With her usual friendliness, Joni told us, "I would like to return to Cuba, I will not forget any of the exciting moments I lived with you. I keep you present in my prayers daily".

Beyond The Seas

I traveled abroad for the first time when I was seven years old. My father wanted Dr. Castro Viejo, an internationally famous ophthalmologist based in New York, to evaluate my brother and me. Dad made an effort to warn us about the good and the bad of that country based on the extensive experience accumulated over the years of his residence there.

I have few memories of that trip, except the visit to Key West and my adventure of going alone to a department store popularly called the Ten Cent.

Located in front of the La Concha Hotel, where we were staying, I had a soda that I ordered in my incipient English. The employee, who did not understand me, spoke to me in Spanish when she realized my lack of knowledge of the language. I will never forget, on the way to New York, a scene that occurred in South Carolina. Poor, very poor neighborhoods where black people lived.

Under persistent rain, the local bus in which we were traveling stopped at the entrance of a "factory" at the time when the workers were leaving. The part of the bus designated for black travelers was overcrowded, and some crossed the mark indicating the space designated for them.

Although there were seats available in the part reserved for white people, the bus driver warned them to either go to their area or get off. Three of them were forced to abandon the vehicle in the rain.

Upon returning to Camagüey on a direct flight from New York City, it seemed to me that I had arrived in a ghost town where there was hardly any movement in the streets.

Living According to the Circumstances

In August 1951, we traveled to the United States again. I was nine years old then. The bus tour was much more impressive for me than the one two years before, with a good number of stops to get to know and rest. I really enjoyed the trip, and even more my father's stories and his insistence on the differences that were not perceptible to my brother and me in that society. I keep in my memory passages, anecdotes and experiences from that trip beyond the sea.

My brother would stay studying high school in a Presbyterian Church facility in Tocoa, south of Atlanta, in the state of Georgia. My brother's study center seemed fabulous to me: it was located between mountains in the middle of the North American countryside, with a waterfall from a crystalline, cold stream.

Many years passed before I traveled beyond the sea again. It was in December 1974 when, at the invitation of the Union of All Baptists of the Soviet Union, I went to that great country in the company of the Reverend Orlando González Carbonell, Baptist pastor in Guantánamo, and the priest Jorge Quintana, also a pastor in the Church of Jacomino, in Havana. It was an unforgettable experience. The attention we received from the Department of International Affairs of that Baptist group was of a high level.

Living According to the Circumstances

In addition to participating in some of the sessions of the Baptist Union assembly, we visited, first Moscow and then Leningrad – today, Saint Petersburg.

We also visited Tbilisi, the capital of Georgia, Abkhazia, and Sochi, as well as places of cultural, historical, and tourist interest. I had the privilege of preaching at the First Baptist Church of Moscow in one of the services on a Sunday in December. I remember the text chosen was from the book of Proverbs 29:18, the same one on which I had based my message in August of that year at the First Baptist Church of Bayamo, then pastored by the Reverend Elmer Lavastida and his faithful companion Gisela Pérez. In Leningrad I spoke in a church about the Baptists in Cuba.

In Tbilisi, I preached again. In the remaining churches, I gave greetings on behalf of the Cuban churches. That country, where I experienced snow and the intensity of the cold, pleasantly surprised me, even when I realized that not everything was as rosy as our hosts wanted us to believe.

In Georgia, we were approached by dissenters from official policy and people begging for alms. At the Union assembly, cracks were evident in the supposed unity that was promoted at all levels of Soviet society.

The Ukrainians argued strongly about the need for an indigenization of worship, which the Russians rejected, wanting it to follow the course of tradition and not knowing the value of a liturgical renewal. The discussion, which we noticed even without understanding it, was not translated by the efficient translator we had, Valentina Ryndina. They hurried us out of the plenary session to go on an unscheduled visit.

My second experience occurred two years later, in 1976. I traveled with the Reverend Héctor Méndez Rodríguez of the Presbyterian Church and, at the time, director of the Youth Program of the Council of Evangelical Churches of Cuba. We traveled to the Continental Assembly of the Latin American Union of Ecumenical Youth (ULAJE) in Ñaña, Peru, located a few kilometers from Lima. We also visited different places in the Peruvian capital, providing me with an accurate image of what Latin America was and its great differences with the political, economic, and social projects of our country. I think that having been in Peru and knowing through the testimony of representatives from other Latin American latitudes, the reality of the South opened my political, ecumenical, and, above all, theological horizons a little more.

Héctor Méndez was a magnificent companion who greatly helped me acquire knowledge and participate more fully in the spheres of the ecumenical movement in Cuba and abroad.

From that assembly, I have maintained friendships to this day with some of the young Peruvians, Argentines, and Uruguayans who were there.

Living According to the Circumstances

My third trip abroad after the triumph of the Revolution was in 1978, to the Caribbean island of Barbados. The Reverend Livio Díaz Rodríguez was, at that time, leader of the Caribbean Christian Conference (CCC) based in Kingston, Jamaica.

Through him, three Cubans – Orlando González, Raimundo García, and Juan A. Tejeda – had already participated in courses at *Codrington College*, a theological institution of the Anglican Church. Knowing the possibility of a new scholarship for a Cuban, I asked Livio to support my application, which he did without delay, and I went to *Codrington College* to study for an entire semester.

The course, called Comunicarib, was sponsored by the Association of Christian Communicators. It was not easy for me to insert myself into it to contribute and learn.

Neither the twenty-four enrolled nor the teachers knew a word of Spanish. On the entire island I was only able to speak in my native language the two times I visited the employees of Cubana de Aviación, the only Cuban representatives and one of the few Spanish speakers residing there at the time. I had to "fight" day and night with English.

The diversity of accents and sometimes the dialects of the everyday speech of my classmates at the College were terrifying to me, but little by little, I was able to understand them, although I am not sure that they understood me.

Living According to the Circumstances

Barbados not only helped me expand my knowledge of English but also to learn about the reality of the Caribbean, which we knew little about and even today we know little about here. I established relationships with local Baptist churches, especially two of them that I went to on Sundays, one in the morning and the other at night. In both, I was able to "preach" in quotes because I am not sure that I did it with the correctness of style and content that I would have liked.

From my stay in Barbados I retain singular anecdotes, which, although complicated, served to make me grow in the midst of the loneliness that overwhelmed me, especially on weekends.

One day when I was returning from Bridgetown, the nation's capital, I encountered a white man of distinguished appearance and apparently English or American fishing in the man-made lake located on the college campus. The man called me and asked me in English if the rector had already returned from his trip to Geneva. I answered him, and noticing my accent, he asked me, "Is your mother tongue French? I ask you because your accent gives you away."

When I explained to him that I was a Spanish speaker, he began to speak perfectly in Spanish. Upon learning that I was Cuban, he showed marked interest. First, we talked about Hemingway, with whom he had hunted in Africa. He told me that he wanted to participate in a marlin fishing tournament in Cuba and that he was "very curious about the Cuban reality," about which he only had information through the media.

He invited me to visit him the following Sunday, "On Sunday, I am going to invite some friends to my house. Some of them speak Spanish, and you will be very happy to be able to speak with them in your language. But I don't know if Fidel authorizes you to visit the house of a gringo who was an officer in the United States Army."

Of course, I accepted, making it clear that I was a citizen free of impositions that prevented me from interacting personally with anyone.

At the appointed time, noon, the man picked me up in his car at the college, and we went to his mansion in the middle of the Barbadian countryside. His "little house" reminded me of those in the southern United States that I had seen in the movie Gone with the Wind. We entered through the kitchen, where his wife, surrounded by a group of black maids, of course, gave precise instructions about what was being prepared. We sat in a small room to talk, and about twenty minutes later, the first guest arrived, Mr. Frank Ortiz, with his wife and his daughter.

When we were introduced, my mind immediately started searching for where I knew this character. As we talked, my mind followed the arduous work of locating him. Ortiz's wife asked me to accompany her, along with her daughter, to tour the mansion's gardens, especially the small zoo owned by my host.

There, she explained to me that they were of Puerto Rican origin and that her daughter wanted to visit Cuba, which her father had always opposed out of fear.

I answered questions about Cuba and encouraged the young woman in her twenties to visit us. In addition, I offered to send her magazines and brochures that I had in my room. When we returned, there were other guests, among them the Venezuelan ambassador in Barbados.

At lunchtime, there were about twenty of us. A white Barbadian, Joan Benjamín, asked me to join her for lunch. Together, we enjoyed the buffet table and talked. She questioned me about Cuba. I think there was no aspect of our culture, politics, economy and religion that she was not interested in. When we finished lunch, many had already left the room and started gatherings in three adjacent areas.

When we said goodbye, Joan Benjamín told me with tremendous discourtesy, "You have been lying to me all the time. Nothing you try to make me believe about your country is true. You are an imposter". I was filled with anger, which I managed to hide at the disrespectful departure of that woman, to whom I politely said goodbye. I later learned that she was the richest woman on the island.

Living According to the Circumstances

I entered a small room where men were talking. When I entered, there was talk of hunts in various parts of the world. My mind kept trying to locate Frank Ortiz. As if to get me out of my musings, he turned to me and asked me if hutias were still abundant in Cuba. Those present did not know this rodent, and Ortiz gave a dissertation about it and how to cook it.

Around five in the afternoon, Mr. Ortiz said goodbye to the owner of the house. He was the first to say goodbye, and he told my host that, as he had to stop by *Codrington College*, he could take me unless I wished to stay a little longer. I accepted, it seemed rude to refuse.

When we were out at the entrance and I was able to see Mr. Ortiz's tremendous car and the driver in the uniform of the United States Army from afar, my mind finally located it. A few months earlier, one of the local newspapers, *The Nation*, had published the news of the presentation of credentials of the new United States ambassador in Barbados: Mr. Frank Ortiz.

In the car, I was sitting in the place that he was supposed to occupy, and that I accepted out of diplomacy, they told me that his daughter had been born in Ethiopia when Ortiz was ambassador there.

The wife asked me, "Mr. Fernández if the Cuban government sends you to fight in Africa like others are doing, would you go?"

Living According to the Circumstances

I thought to myself, "This is getting bad!" I responded, "In Cuba, participating in what we call solidarity with Africa is optional for each person on a voluntary basis. I am a man of peace, and I would gladly go to Africa or any place in the world to work for peace with justice, just as I have learned from the Gospel."

The topic of conversation was changed to talk about Hemingway's literary works.

A month later, Frank Ortiz and his wife attended celebrations at the *College*. They recognized me, and the rector sat me at the presidential table next to them.

In his greeting message to begin the banquet, he said that he had the privilege of sitting next to a representative of the United States and a Cuban as a preamble to a world of peace and understanding among all human beings.

When the dance began after the banquet, Mrs. Ortiz asked me to give her the first piece. My fellow students then wanted to lynch me, "How did you agree to the rector's farce?"

In Barbados, I managed to obtain a passing grade in my course, which stimulated me a lot.

Some years later, reading the Hilo Directo section of the Granma newspaper, I was surprised by a piece of news. "Mr. Frank Ortiz has been appointed ambassador of the United States in Argentina. Various national institutions that fight for human rights have protested the presence in our country of a renowned agent of the United States Central Intelligence Agency, CIA."

In July 1979, I had the privilege of being invited by the Baptist Convention of Nicaragua. In my capacity as general secretary of the Baptist Student Workers Coordination of Cuba, I visited that country during the celebration of the first anniversary of the triumph of the Sandinista Revolution. I had the joy of traveling with Joel Suárez Rodés, who was in his second year of high school. It was shocking to see myself accompanied by a teenager with a culture far superior to the average of his generation. I have no doubt that the education received from his father, the Reverend Raúl Suárez Ramos, and his mother, Clara Rodés González, had achieved its goals. My companion soon made his own agenda and made his way not only among Baptists but in the evangelical world and in other spheres of civil and governmental society.

There, I met Dr. Juan Stan, the friendly and supportive American naturalized Costa Rican. He owned a deep knowledge of the book of Revelation, of which he wrote quite a bit. From Stan, whom we welcomed in Cuba and even at Emmanuel Church during my pastorate, I learned a lot on that occasion and afterwards.

The relationships with Dr. Gustavo Parajón, ecumenical leader, Baptist pastor, and notable doctor, helped me a lot to learn about the culture, tradition, and history of that sister nation.

I participated in meetings with leaders of the Evangelical Alliance for Development (CEPAD), founded after the earthquake that destroyed Managua, and which continued its work, first humanist, evangelical, and supportive, and later as a meeting place and ecumenical realization.

But, without a doubt, the highlight of my stay in Nicaragua was the celebrations for the first anniversary of its revolution. That square filled with men and women overflowed with palpitating joy when our president, Fidel Castro, entered. My heart tightened with emotion, I don't deny it. God had granted me the privilege of being in the Plaza de la Revolución in Cuba to celebrate the first anniversary of the Revolution, and now he granted me the same privilege, but in a plaza in Managua.

At the Baptist Seminary, where we spent the night, the Reverend Francisco Rodés worked temporarily as a professor who was accompanied by his wife, Lila González. They helped me establish relationships of fellowship and fraternity with the Baptist Convention of Nicaragua, ties that were maintained for many years and through which many Baptist leaders, especially related to COEBAC, traveled to that country to help churches, Baptist or not, in training to live the faith in a revolutionary process. There were also many pastors and Baptist leaders from that country who accompanied us in the National Camps on Christian Social Responsibility, organized every July by COEBAC in different places in our country.

In the 1980s, I traveled to various places in Latin America, completing invitations of various kinds. Relevant was the participation in Mexico City – also representing COEBAC – in the international event Christian Personalities of Latin America for the Rights of the People, organized by the Reverend Eunice Santana and the Reverend Alberto González, from PRISA, the Puerto Rican ecumenical organization.

From that same decade, another impact activity was the one organized by ULAJE and carried out in Panama: Human Rights, People's Rights. The highlight was the presence of Carlos Zenón, a Puerto Rican fighter who, in his small fishing boat based on the island of Vieques, had challenged the North American navy, demanding the right of the Puerto Ricans to have the marines abandon their island and return the territory which they had converted into an air-naval base.

It was not until July 1987 that I had the privilege of returning to the United States again. I did it to represent COEBAC at the meeting of the *Baptist Peace Fellowship of North America*. It was the second of those meetings, and it took place in the state of North Carolina at the *Mars Hill College* facilities.

Living According to the Circumstances

The *College*, located among the mountains next to a small, typically American town of the same name, was an ideal setting for the meeting.

Despite having participated in so many events in various places around the world, it was the most supportive, fraternal, and profound of those I have had the opportunity to attend.

The Reverend Ken Sehested, then general secretary of that movement, was and has continued to be, very supportive of Cuba and its project. I had the chance of presenting one night in the *College* temple a report on the objectives, projects, and actions of the COEBAC, which was followed by countless questions that extended that activity for more than an hour.

Later, in 1996, I visited Mars Hill College again, where I preached.

Also worth remembering were the events organized by the Conference of Baptists for Peace in Sweden, Canada, Nicaragua, and Italy. They all had great scope and content, which contributed greatly to delineating our theological position and to gaining relationships with Baptists from all latitudes who, with marked coincidences with our efforts and dreams, were united in a common struggle.

From the one carried out in Sweden in July 1988, I have a memory of the relationships that arose with Dr. Roger Crook and his wife, Mary Ruth. The professor was retired from

Meredith College in North Carolina and a Baptist minister, and she was a retired professor of English Literature.

Later, in the summer of 1989, the Reverend Francisco Rodés and I went to the Crook home to spend several months with them and, in parallel, take a summer course at the *Wake Technological School* that served both of us to improve our knowledge of the English language. The Crooks not only sheltered and fed us, but with them, and through them, we were able to get to know North American society from the inside.

Without it being in my plans, I had the opportunity to serve global ecumenism through my participation in three tasks of the World Council of Churches.

The first – which I will refer to in more detail in another chapter – was the Ecumenical Network in Defense of People with Disabilities (EDAN), of which I was the coordinator for Latin America for eighteen years and, for ten, a member of its coordination group.

In the period between 1998 and 2007, I was a member of the Justice, Peace and Integrity of Creation (JPC) unit. In the next stage of the WCC (2007-2013), I was elected to join its Commission on International Affairs (CCIA), an important sphere of the largest ecumenical movement in the world. In that commission I joined two work areas, first that of Social Justice and then the working group on Religious Freedom.

Living According to the Circumstances

This last activity was the most attractive of all and in which I felt most fulfilled. I remember that at the first meeting in that area, I proposed holding the next meeting in Cuba, which was accepted, although for political reasons, there were those who did not attend.

With that meeting, which was held at the Evangelical Theology Seminary, the working group recognized the freedom of religion that we Cubans enjoy, and comments that were still circulating in some mass media were denied. The visits to China and Albania, which I consider the most relevant to the Commission's work, allowed me to gain in-depth knowledge of the hopes and frustrations of Christians in both countries.

At first, even though we were provided with sufficient information, I felt that they still had a long way to go to ensure that the equalization of opportunities and the free determination of the different factors committed to faith reached an adequate level.

To be frank, I got the impression that the Chinese Communist Party's years of isolation, rejection, and confrontation with believers were not completely over. I thanked God that our experience under the political leadership of the Cuban Communist Party would not have had even remotely the same connotations.

Living According to the Circumstances

When we evaluated the Chinese situation, we thanked God for the great difference that exists with our country, which, without becoming the Kingdom of God on earth, is much closer to the project of justice and freedom that God in Jesus Christ has made known to us.

I think that the situation in Albania was also pitiful. After a strict autocracy under the leadership of Enver Hoxha, who is still remembered with gratitude by some sectors, which I found difficult to understand, the Orthodox Church, with great power and vast wealth, has become a power and created an enormous abyss between it and the different, but thriving, Christian groups of other aspects. Some of them say they are marginalized, and even the most fundamentalists feel persecuted. I was not able to find out the veracity of the accusations, but the Orthodox Church has religious power and is an ally of political power.

A planned visit to Turkey was going to give me the opportunity to present a document, which I wrote and translated into English, on religious freedom in Cuba. The lack of a transit visa through France, which I did not apply for due to lack of knowledge, prevented me from assessing the religious situation in Turkish lands, which excited me.

Indonesia, where I went twice, was another stop of my work with the working group on religious freedom in the world. That country, predominantly Muslim, allows, to a certain extent –

although violent confrontations occur from time to time – freedom of belief.

Hearing the mosques call to prayer at certain times of the day and night, getting to know at close hand the feelings of Muslims and Christians in a country with a tradition different from ours, was shocking. The Christians with whom we interacted did not report seeing themselves persecuted or marginalized, but they did yearn for more possibilities of action and dreamed of the methods and procedures of the so-called Christian countries.

My second trip to Indonesia, in February 2014, was due to my involvement in *Action Church Together* (ACT). This thriving global ecumenical movement had contacted me at the suggestion of the *Church World Service* to be the leader of its Disability Community of Practice. I was very hesitant to accept that responsibility because I felt incompetent to carry it out.

In the end, I accepted because of the strong and exemplary work carried out by the Pastoral Care of People with Disabilities, a program of the Council of Churches of Cuba. For a year and a half, I carried out that responsibility, but at our first meeting, held in Indonesia, I felt compelled to request that I be relieved of the position.

The ACT demanded much more than I could provide, not only because of my lack of a broader knowledge of the English language but because of the amount of time I would have to dedicate to it.

I very much regretted that decision, but I learned in ecumenical work that one should never take on something for which one is not well prepared.

Accompanied by the Reverend Manuel Delgado, at the time executive secretary of the Fraternity of Baptist Churches of Cuba, I represented that organization at a meeting of Caribbean Baptists held on the island of Grand Bahamas, in the archipelago of the same name north of Cuba. I have always felt a very special affection for the Caribbean, and that event captivated me not only because of its color and its expressive and catchy music but also because of the sense of brotherhood of the participants. I have greatly regretted not having done everything possible for a greater approach, personally and institutionally, with the churches, Baptist or not, of the Caribbean.

Perhaps the fact of having spent a semester studying at *Codrington College* in Barbados, among people from different Caribbean territories, awakened my love for that part of the world.

As part of my responsibilities at EDAN, I attended two events in the Caribbean, one in Jamaica and the other in Curacao.

Living According to the Circumstances

Together with Dr. Samuel Kabue, general coordinator of EDAN, I once visited Jamaica and Trinidad and Tobago. Over there I learned and shared with churches and institutions related to the issue of disability.

My time in the United States was not limited to my childhood trips with my parents and brother and participation in the meeting of the Baptist Peace Fellowship in Mars Hill in 1987. I also made frequent trips to Monroe, Louisiana, as part of Emmanuel Baptist Church's exchange with its sister church, *Northminster*. It is worth noting that this brotherhood between both churches was not only a possibility to visit them or be visited but an arena of fellowship and service that has greatly contributed to the formation of both communities of faith.

Accompanied by Reverend Adalberto Cuéllar, I participated in two assemblies of the Progressive Baptist Convention of the United States.

That Baptist group, of which the Reverend Martin Luther King Jr. was a part, always expressed its interest in a closer relationship with the Fraternity of Baptist Churches of Cuba. Together with the Reverend Estela Hernández, then President of FIBAC, I participated in the city of Washington DC in an assembly of the Alliance of Baptists of North America, which I later repeated together with Ormara in 2019.

Living According to the Circumstances

I dreamed of visiting three countries: Australia, Germany, and Argentina. The first one was out of my reach, but I was in Germany twice. My impression was not very pleasant: a very uncommunicative society, extremely organized and not at all hospitable, although I had some positive experiences.

I considered that two visits, both, of course, for work, were enough. Argentina was a childhood dream: a great-aunt, sister of my maternal grandmother, Emma Pérez Guzmán, had lived in that country. Emma – although it is not right to tell it – left her husband and two daughters in Camagüey, where she lived, at the end of the 1920s because she fell in love with a Roman Catholic priest with whom she went on an adventure to that South American country.

Once the romance ended, Emma suffered many hardships, work, and poverty, and only thanks to the help of my uncle Enrique Collot, then representative to the Chamber for the province of Camagüey, she was able to return to Cuba, although not to the heart of her deteriorated and damaged family.

These stories of "impossible romances" were never told at home in front of the children, but Emma did narrate her beautiful Argentine experiences without telling us about the difficulties and deprivations.

Living According to the Circumstances

Argentina, therefore, was a childhood dream. I was in that country twice: the first as part of my work as coordinator for Latin America of EDAN; the second to participate in the assembly of the Latin American Council of Churches. The experiences satisfied me. I had a good reception among the Argentinians with whom I interacted. I enjoyed the typical dishes and the culture of the country, but it did not become the Argentina of my dreams. Maybe because Libertad Lamarque and Juan Domingo Perón were no longer there, or because *Billiken*, the beautifully illustrated magazine that was not missing in my home, no longer existed.

I have been left with the dissatisfaction of not having known more about Africa, as I would have liked. Zimbabwe was the first African country I visited due to the eighth assembly of the World Council of Churches being held there, where the project to create the Ecumenical Network in Defense of People with Disabilities was born. My other African experience was my three visits to Kenya, where I traveled for my responsibilities in EDAN, a WCC program that had its seat in Nairobi, the Kenyan capital, throughout its existence. I don't forget that I made my first visit to that African country alone.

At that time, Cuba did not have diplomatic relations with Kenya, so the entry visa was placed on the airline on which I was traveling, which in that case was British Airways. I spoke days before my trip to that remote country with the person in charge of the line in Havana, who confirmed that he had the visa in his possession.

On the scheduled day, two friends accompanied me to the José Martí airport, and at my request, they left me alone there. When the British check-in counter opened, I was the first to be served. The employees did not have the visa. The line manager was traveling that same night back from England on the flight I was supposed to board, and when I boarded it, it was late because the flight had already been closed.

"You can't travel without your visa, we're very sorry," the employee told me curtly. I argued, but his cavalier response was, "I already told you what was happening, please get off the counter because you are disturbing the other people." You can imagine my mortification. By hitting the cane, I managed, with the help of a person, to leave the airport premises, take a taxi, and return that same night to Ciego de Ávila. Upon arriving home, Ormara, surprised, told me that they had called me from Kenya, insisting on the importance of my presence there and warning that they were waiting for me.

Early in the morning, I decided to go to the Immigration and Foreigners offices of the Ministry of the Interior in Ciego de Ávila. Fortunately, a senior official from the bureau who was visiting Havana told me that I could travel without a visa if I had the round-trip ticket with me. We went to the Cubana de Aviación offices without hope of achieving anything, but the efficient employee who assisted us told us that at ten at night, there was a Cubana flight to London, and nine hours later a British flight to Nairobi and that there were seats available in both of them. We booked them, and Ormara suggested taking me to the airport with the help of Lázaro Monzón, a member of our church, so I could fulfill my commitment. We arrived at Rancho Boyeros in time to board, and I passed immigration control without any problem.

The difficulty arose in the nine hours of waiting that I had to spend in London in an airport full of people where, curiously, no one spoke English or Spanish: it seemed like an imitation of the Babel Tower. The employee who assisted me when I got off the Cubana de Aviación flight helped me settle into a seat near the "rest room," where I settled in and slept a lot. An hour before taking the flight, I tried to go to the British check-in counter to find out about the continuity of my trip. It was impossible for me. How can a blind man move with only the help of his cane in an unknown place?

Stumbling, I tried, but no one batted an eye. And, furthermore, how could I communicate if I didn't hear anyone speaking in one of the only two languages in which I could make myself understood?

Finally, as a saving grace, someone spoke English, and I asked for help. I arrived at the check-in counter, and upon my questions, they told me that the flight was an hour late. Another hour! There would be ten in London.

Already on the plane, starving, thirsty, and sleepy, I fell asleep. I woke up in the middle of a profound silence. They had already distributed the food! I called the flight attendant, who brought me a VERY appetizing dish, which, whatever it was, I devoured hungrily.

The "good thing" came later when I arrived in Nairobi. First, it took me a long time to look for the visa to be put in my passport and then search for the luggage, which did not arrive, and for which I waited until the last day of my stay in that country when it finally arrived.

The worst was when I finally left the airport with the person who assisted me and whose English was inaccessible to me due to his Kenyan accent. Nobody expected me. I finally found a phone number in one of my notes. We called, but it turned out to be a FAX.

There, I verified that I did not suffer from a heart condition. Very calmly, I wrote a FAX, and we sent it. After another hour, we had a response. They would come look for me, but it was very far, and it would take two more hours. Then, like so many other times, I said to myself, "I will never travel anywhere alone again." I haven't completed it, apparently I have a bad memory.

Living According to the Circumstances

In another sense, that trip was very positive. We consolidated the creation of EDAN, and they appointed me coordinator for Latin America, a task that has consumed a lot of my time and my nervous energy but which, without a doubt, has been a blessing.

During the stay in Kenya, the meeting participants organized a safari. Everyone was interested in visiting a national park where African fauna species abounded. Someone told me, "You're not going to go, are you? After all, what will you be able to see?"

That segregation bothered me, and, of course, then, with more enthusiasm, I decided to participate in the safari. When they talked about big, tall giraffes, I could see them in my imagination much bigger than my companions.

And, of course, the hippos that were in the lake were much more gigantic than the ones my companions saw. The lions roared, and we could all hear their sound, but the manes of the lions that I "saw" were much more lush than the ones the rest of the group saw.

In short, I think I enjoyed the safari much more than those who discussed that unforgettable experience with me. Many years after that walk through the African jungles, I still "see" the same beautiful images.

There is no doubt that God always has a blessing for his sons and daughters in the midst of diversity.

I thank God because, over a few years I was able to have great experiences beyond the sea. All of them, in one way or another, provided me with knowledge, experiences, and relationships that have been very valuable in my life.

I also thank him for having participated, always as an advisor, in three assemblies of the World Council of Churches: Zimbabwe (1998); Porto Alegre, Brazil (2007); and Buzan, South Korea (2013).

Below, I list the countries that I have visited, some more than once, always for work reasons:

Asia- Philippines, Thailand, South Korea, Indonesia and China

Africa - Kenya and Zimbabwe.

North America - Canada, United States and Mexico

Central America - El Salvador, Costa Rica, Nicaragua and Panama

South America - Colombia, Ecuador, Peru, Bolivia, Chile, Argentina, Uruguay and Brazil

The Caribbean - Bahamas, Haiti, Dominican Republic, Jamaica, Barbados, Trinidad and Tobago,

Living According to the Circumstances

Curacao, Puerto Rico, Turks and Caicos and US Virgin Islands

Europe - Portugal, Spain, France, Switzerland, Italy, Vatican City, Albania, Greece, Russia, Georgia, Czechoslovakia, Poland, Germany, Sweden, Norway, Holland and Belgium

The Ecumenical Network In Defense Of The People With Disabilities (EDAN)

I had learned from information in bulletins and other media of the manifest interest of the World Council of Churches (WCC) in incorporating the issue of disability into its programs. I learned about the work done in this regard by Lynda Katsuno, from Canada, who had worked at the WCC headquarters some years before.

One day, when pastor Orestes González was president of the Council of Churches of Cuba, I was told I was invited to a meeting in Geneva on the topic of disability. Dr. Ofelia Ortega had suggested my name as a possible participant in that meeting.

At that time, it was a Korean woman, Yi Ya Li, who worked as coordinator of the project carried out by the WCC on the subject, a job that ceased a year and a half after the aforementioned activity due to financial difficulties. That meeting was, for me, like a breakthrough on the international level regarding disability. I met people with whom I exchanged and worked until the end of my responsibilities at the WCC.

Then, in 1998, I was invited to attend the eighth assembly of the World Council of Churches in Harare, Zimbabwe. About twenty people with disabilities from different parts of the world and from different confessions were selected as advisors to this summit event of world ecumenism.

Initially we were placed in a tent, where it was intended for us blind people to read in Braille and for others to do manual labor, in short, for us to make ourselves known during the assembly as exhibits in a zoo. We didn't have to wait long for the group of advisors to meet and dismantle the project of activities that they had planned for us.

Having radically rejected the initial plans, we began a program of insertion into the different activities of the assembly. We even drew up strategies to make it known that what was missing was inclusion and not pity or paternalism. That transformative purpose achieved its objectives, and by the end of the assembly, many people had changed their way of thinking.

In a meeting held by the group, we decided that we should organize ourselves to achieve inclusion in the WCC based on our own experiences, demands, and needs. This is how we chose Brother Samuel Kabue, a blind person from Kenya who worked as program director at the National Council of Churches in that country. Mr. Kabue would represent us and call for a new meeting as soon as funding was obtained for it.

A year later, in Nairobi, Kenya, what was called the *Ecumenical Disability Advocacy Network*, EDAN, was born, with the presence of those of us who had previously met in Harare and other people with disabilities from various countries and Christian denominations.

At the meeting, it was decided to divide the work of the network into the same eight regions in which the WCC carries out its work: Asia, Pacific, Europe, the Middle East, Africa, North America, the Caribbean, and Latin America. I was appointed EDAN coordinator for Latin America. I considered that the experience accumulated in Cuba through the work we did with the Pastoral Care of People with Disabilities, a program of the Council of Churches of Cuba, would help me in the new responsibility, and it did.

We carried out a brief investigation into the situation of people with disabilities in Latin America and found a bleak panorama, especially in relation to the action of the Churches in favor of the inclusion of this population sector in their programs, activities, and responsibilities.

At that time, 1999, the Methodist Church in Mexico had a program called Living Stones, whose objective was to encourage churches to accommodate and fulfill possibilities for people with disabilities.

Unfortunately, this program disappeared after a few years of existence due to a lack of financial resources.

Living According to the Circumstances

In Uruguay, the Waldensian Church had an institution in operation to care for people with intellectual disabilities. It was, and still is, a good initiative, but it leaned heavily towards welfare. In the south of Brazil, in Rio Grande do Sul, the Evangelical Church of the Lutheran Confession developed a magnificent program with which it encouraged the churches of its denomination to work for the inclusion of people with disabilities in their actions.

As far as we knew, it was a very complete program and well accepted among the Lutheran churches in the country. For their part, in many of the countries of South America – Argentina, Colombia, Peru, Chile, among others – the Baptist conventions linked to the work of the Southern Baptist Convention were beginning evangelistic work, or rather, evangelizer, with deaf people.

Finally, in Venezuela, there was a good ministry with deaf people in one of the main churches in Caracas, Emmanuel Baptist Church, thanks to which even a deaf woman had carried out theological studies and created a strong ministry in that church with outreach to other deaf people in the city.

The same thing happened in the First Baptist Church of San Salvador, El Salvador, where, at the initiative of a father with two deaf children, a consistent ministry with deaf people had been developed, also focused on evangelistic action.

There was no doubt that Latin America needed more concrete action and, especially, that the patterns of welfare and religious proselytism be abandoned to make way for inclusion programs that would allow people with disabilities to be subjects of their own actions and function in the life of their communities of faith with autonomy, responding to the vocation and call of God.

With this orientation, we held in Quito, Ecuador, in June 2001, a first event under the banner of EDAN, the first Consultation on Disability: Role of the Churches, Future Strategies.

Representatives of the Episcopal Church of Brazil attended it, already with experience in that task; the Lutheran Church of the state of Rio Grande do Sul; and people with disabilities from Nicaragua and Venezuela.

The executive secretary of the Latin American Council of Churches, Reverend Israel Batista, accompanied us and showed interest in what, as EDAN, we promised to do.

Thanks to the understanding and solidarity of Sister Marta Palma, from Chile, who at that time was the coordinator of the WCC program for Latin America, we obtained new resources to travel to Ecuador and begin interesting work with the indigenous churches of that country, aimed at including the issue of disability in their agendas.

Living According to the Circumstances

For ten years we worked with these congregations with magnificent results that allowed a change in the understanding of the issue of disability.

The first consultation was followed by others: São Leopoldo, Rio Grande do Sul, in September 2002; Cárdenas, Cuba, in 2004; Córdoba, Argentina, in October 2006; Quito, Ecuador, in March 2008; San Salvador, El Salvador, in November 2010; Bogotá, Colombia, in 2011; Santiago de Chile, Chile, in October 2012.

A specific objective that guided the work of the Network in Latin America was to promote the curricular inclusion of disability in theological institutions.

With that end, promotional activities and visits were carried out to several of them: Semisud, from Ecuador; Baptist Polytechnic University (UPOLI), of Nicaragua; Latin American Biblical Seminary, in San José, Costa Rica; Higher Institute of Theological Studies (ISEDET), in Buenos Aires, Argentina; São Leopoldo Seminary, Rio Grande do Sul, Brazil; Baptist Seminary of Montevideo, Uruguay; Presbyterian Seminary of Lima, Peru; Evangelical Seminary of Theology, Matanzas, Cuba; Eastern Cuba Baptist Seminary, Santiago de Cuba, Cuba; Universidad Bautista de Cali, Colombia. Not everyone joined the efforts promoted by EDAN, but, as in the parable, "the seed was sown" and has germinated in the Baptist Seminary of Santiago de Cuba, the Evangelical Seminary of

Theology in Matanzas, Semisud of Quito, the Higher Institute of Theological Studies of Buenos Aires, the Bible University of Latin America in San José, among others.

A significant effort by EDAN was the work carried out in Haiti. A Cuban couple with a family history that linked them to that country trained in Cuba to serve as "missionaries" on the issue of disability in the poorest nation on the continent.

First, they had the help of Brother Manuel Quintero in his capacity as coordinator of *Interfrontiers in Mission* for four years and later, with the support of the *Church World Service* and with the collaboration in the country of CONASEPH (National Spiritual Council of the Churches of Haiti), and later of the Christian Service of Haiti.

For seven years, both worked to understand the need to include people with disabilities in the life of the Haitian evangelical and/or Protestant Churches. The goal was to discard the pity and paternalism of the action of Christian congregations, to look for alternatives for a better life for people with disabilities, and in cooperation with governmental and non-governmental bodies to implement an adequate and inclusive policy for them.

A group of eleven young people from the country were trained through workshops and short courses to give continuity to the program. This became even stronger after the terrible earthquake that hit the Haitian capital. It served as a frame of reference for various cooperation agencies that, through our "missionaries," reached the most dispossessed with material, spiritual, and/or medical aid.

The work that began in 2006 with the arrival of our two collaborators in Port-au-Prince was unfortunately cut short in 2013 when they, without consultation, dedicated themselves to other tasks, ignoring their responsibilities and abandoning a task that we enjoyed so much.

At the initiative of Dr. Elsa Tamez, work was carried out to translate biblical texts into the Costa Rican sign language, in which the deaf community of that country was adequately prepared under the orientation and guidance of Dr. Tamez.

This work spread to other places in the region: Colombia, Argentina, and Cuba. EDAN joined this task from the beginning and was greatly benefited from the cooperation of the well-known Latin American biblical scholar who, from her efforts to know and work with deaf people, went on to collaborate with other people with disabilities and become part of EDAN's actions throughout Latin America.

For more efficient work of EDAN in our region, it was divided into the same regions in which CLAI works on the continent. In each of them, there was a coordinator: Rio de la Plata, Norberto Rash; Andina, Alexandra Meneses;

Mesoamerica, Fabián Gutiérrez; Gran Caribe, Rolando Verdecia; and Brazil, Lara Müller. They all put their efforts and capabilities at the service of the network's objectives in their areas of influence.

On two occasions, Buenos Aires was the scene of important interreligious meetings: Muslims, Jews, and Christians (evangelicals, Orthodox, and Catholics) met to jointly analyze the issue of disability and the understanding of it from each of their religious cultures.

In November 2009, a meeting of young Christians with disabilities was held in Puembo, Ecuador, attended by young people from Costa Rica, Nicaragua, Ecuador, Peru, Argentina, Brazil, the Dominican Republic, and Cuba.

EDAN made it possible for the Emmanuel trio to take their music to Ecuador in September 2004. These three visually impaired people, living in the easternmost of the Cuban provinces, had come together to perform Christian music with Cuban and Caribbean rhythms, all of their own inspiration.

Bringing that music to the Andean nation was a dream for those three brethren, but also for the Pastoral Care of People with Disabilities of the Council of Churches of Cuba, to which EDAN joined with the resources and organization in Ecuador.

Both in Quito and in several places in the provinces of Chimborazo and Pichincha, some of the places visited were purely indigenous. Emmanuel made the attendees vibrate with joy and movement. The evangelical radio station La Voz de Los Andes interviewed the members of the trio and dedicated a program to disseminating their art, something that an evangelical television network also did.

The Network, convinced of the need to achieve an understanding of the issue of disability from a theological approach, held events for that purpose. The first of them was held in Quito in March 2008 under the title of First Latin American Consultation on Theology and Disability.

In November 2010, San Salvador hosted a second activity aimed at including the issue of disability in the Churches and theological institutions of Mesoamerica. The valuable materials resulting from both events were published in the form of books entitled *First Latin American Consultation on Theology and Disability* and *Como una sola flor seremos*, respectively.

The first was translated into English and Portuguese. These two significant efforts were followed by two more, one in Bogotá and another in Santiago de Chile in October 2012.

On two occasions, EDAN has managed to bring together Christian women with disabilities from Latin America to reflect on the marginalization, discrimination, and rejection of which they are victims. In the traditional Latin American context, women occupy a very secondary place in society and even in the Churches, but if these women are also indigenous or Afro-descendant, the marginalization is greater. And, of course, if living with a disability is added to these two elements, the effect is immense.

Faced with this situation, the Network has carried out various tasks, but the two meetings of women with disabilities have been very significant. Both took place at the Christian Center for Reflection and Dialogue of the Presbyterian Church in the city of Cárdenas, Cuba. The first, of which one publication emerged, was held in 2008, and the second in 2016.

The evaluation that the Network on a global scale has made of the work in Latin America has been very satisfactory, which made it possible for me to join the EDAN coordinating group for ten years.

In October 2014, during the meeting of regional coordinators held in Holland, I stepped down from my responsibility as coordinator for Latin America. Dr. Samuel Kabue, general coordinator of the program, had invited those of us who served as regional coordinators and had been in leadership roles for a long time to give up our positions to younger people.

In the case of Latin America, Sister Alexandra Meneses, from Ecuador, was proposed and accepted without hesitation, who, since the beginning of the work in this part of the world, had joined with enthusiasm and demonstrated her capacity.

Living According to the Circumstances

Native Peoples In Latin America

I have always experienced deep pain for the genocide carried out by Spanish colonialism against the defenseless population originating from the Cuban archipelago. I read with care and extreme interest everything published by anthropologists, historians, and researchers on pre-Columbian cultures in Cuba. But it was the History of America book, written by Enrique Collot Jiménez, a study text in the fifth year of high school in the 1950s, that allowed me to delve into the knowledge of the life of the native peoples in the rest of Latin America.

My first contact with these magnificent cultures occurred when I went to Nicaragua for the first time in 1980, invited by the Baptist Convention of that country.

One of the events that was held was the Second Interdenominational Retreat of Evangelical Pastors of Nicaragua (RIPEN). A good number of pastors and evangelical leaders from the Miskito ethnic group and a few from the Sumu attended. I had the opportunity to share a dormitory with some of them.

Although verbal communication was not the best, due to their lack of knowledge of my Spanish and my total lack of mastery of their Spanish, I learned about their ancestral difficulties and the hopes they placed in the future that was beginning in that country.

My relations with the Miskitos intensified when I established working relations with the Reverend Marcelo Borges, Moravian, Miskito, and the blind pastor. With Reverend Borges, I deepened my knowledge and increased my love for forgotten and mistreated people.

The Atlantic coast of Nicaragua and Honduras was a very different territory from the rest of both countries, populated mainly by the two indigenous peoples mentioned above, plus the Rama ethnic group and the Garifunas, descendants of the black Antillean population settled there centuries before.

The next experience was my visit to the Anthropological Museum of Mexico City in 1980, to which I returned on another occasion years later. There I learned, in a full day of tour, about the Aztec and Mayan cultures. Standing in front of the Aztec calendar moved me. How much knowledge was despised, outraged, and unknown by the Spanish conquerors!

On that trip, I was invited by Pastor Lázaro González and his wife, Olivia de González, to exchange and preach in the indigenous churches under the guidance and orientation of CICEM, an institution that brought together, with its own leadership, the churches made up of participants from the native peoples.

Living According to the Circumstances

A subsequent trip to Mexico in 1993 allowed me to reach evangelical communities made up of indigenous Oaxacans. I spent the night in their houses, preached in their churches and learned their customs.

However, the most complete experience of working with indigenous peoples was the sustained work carried out with Quechua men and women from Ecuador.

I met one of them in 1989, at the Latin American Evangelical Seminary in San José, Costa Rica, when I was invited to teach a short course on the task of disability. Brother Jerónimo Yantalema was a student at the institution and invited me to visit him in Ecuador.

I took him at his word, and in the year 2000 I traveled with Ormara to a camp located in Colta, Chimborazo, to work with the participants on the topic of inclusion of people with disabilities in the life of Ecuadorian indigenous churches.

Colta was a great challenge for both of us. The conditions of the place were extremely inhospitable for our customs and culture, to which was added a hostile environment due to temperature and altitude. We had to grow in the face of difficulties.

We realized that the participants did not easily understand our Caribbean Spanish, we had to change the teaching method and be more expressive, theatrical, and dynamic. We achieved communication on the second day of our stay there, and along with the communication a very favorable flow of affection.

The guide of the work among Quechua people with disabilities was brother César Yumi, who had lost his sight in a work accident, and since then, amid sacrifices and deprivations, he had dedicated himself to teaching, encouraging, and helping indigenous people with visual disability. His life was an inspiration for everyone, and especially for us, who valued what Yumi was capable of doing in the complicated and difficult situations in which he worked.

Twice, we managed to have César Yumi accompany us in Cuba and share with people with disabilities from the Cuban Churches his vast experience, his spiritual strength, and his dreams and commitments.

Ten beautiful years followed that "baptismal" experience. Year after year, sometimes more than once, we returned to Chimborazo: workshops, meetings, courses, visits, exchanges took us into the world of Quechua culture and opened possibilities for them to accept disability not as a curse, punishment or consequence of sin, but as one more form of manifestation of the multiform human existence.

We witnessed how a young Quechua man, Angel Guamán, imposed himself on his family, traditions, ancestral culture and, being blind, under the pastoral and educational guidance of

César Yumi, began studies that led him to graduate first as a lawyer and then held a doctorate in law.

Guamán was a beautiful example of the tenacity and perseverance of a person who, in adverse circumstances, prevails and achieves his goals.

It is also worth mentioning the work we do with aboriginal populations in the Urban and Rural Mission Coalition (MUR/EDAN). Brother Oscar Bravo, from Peru, challenged us to work on the issue of disability with indigenous populations from Ecuador, Peru and Bolivia. This work carried out in two years of intense activity, gave us great satisfaction when we saw how the leaders of the churches that grouped these brothers and sisters felt motivated to understand disability as part of divine creativity and not as a punishment and curse.

I consider that the debt we have with the native peoples has not been paid. The "Christianization" initiated by Catholicism in the colonial era was followed, although with different methods, by the different waves of missionaries sent by the agencies of the Northern Churches. They considered their original beliefs, their extreme love of Pachamama, the sun, the air, and nature diabolical.

As Catholicism did before, they imposed a white, blonde, and light-eyed God.

Living According to the Circumstances

In rejection of this penetration, the Quechua indigenous people of Ecuador expelled the foreign missionaries from their territories in the mid-1960s.

Contrary to the missionaries' belief that the Christian faith would disappear from the indigenous territory, it was solidified with the action of pastors, missionaries, and leaders of the Ecuadorian Indigenous Church.

Of course, their customs imposed a new reality and a new spirituality. Today, these congregations, all under Quechua's direction and administration, continue to grow in Ecuador, Bolivia, and Peru.

The Methodist Church of Bolivia sparked my interest. Its bishop during the period of our relations was an indigenous Aymara whose brother was ambassador of his country in Denmark under the government of the Movement towards Socialism (MAS).

I shared with that Church on two occasions and verified that it respected the culture, tradition, and idiosyncrasy of the native cultures of Bolivia. It must be remembered that this plurinational State is made up of thirty-seven different ethnic groups.

Latin American Christians have a great debt to our original ancestors. I believe that it is essential to think about ways, means, and procedures through which we learn from their cultures, traditions, and beliefs.

Living According to the Circumstances

My Four Pastors

It may seem incredible, but in my long existence, at least until the moment of writing these lines, I have had the spiritual guidance of only four pastors, all very different from each other.

Rafael M. Gregorich Escalona (1900-1967)

When I was born in 1942, the church of my parents had been pastored for more than ten years by the Reverend Rafael M. Gregorich Escalona, who had previously ministered in the church of Jatibonico in Camagüey territory. Gregorich came from the church of Jibacoa, a territory that was part of the municipality of Manzanillo in the vicinity of the Sierra Maestra.

Married to Consuelo Sánchez Paneque, a native of Manzanillo, he had eight children: Rafael, Amparo (who died as a child), Isis, Luis, Rubén, Consuelito, Juan Enrique and David.

The members of the pastoral family with which I grew up at the First Baptist Church of Camagüey were very different from each other, but they were all characterized by the brotherhood and companionship that they had learned from their elders. That pastoral house was a space for all of us who were part of the congregation.

Consuelo told me that, as a child, my parents did not allow me to go to the parsonage to play when they or my grandmother took me to church activities, "They never let you come and play with Juan Enrique or David before, during or after the services." It was true, my parents told me that this house was as private as ours and that there was no reason to bother them.

On occasions, I would play with Kike or David, but never during activities. They also came to play at my house sometimes.

When I grew up, I forgot the lesson they had given me as a child, and the gatherings we had in the interior portals or the dining room of the parsonage were long.

Sometimes, all the residents of the house would go to their rooms little by little, and the youth would stay talking, singing, telling stories. There were times when Consuelito, who often, along with Rubén, was one of the last to go to bed, told us, "Whoever leaves last, make sure the door is closed properly."

Grego, as we lovingly called our pastor, was all love, and the education on which he based his teaching was a projection of 1 Corinthians 13. That biblical passage, in the translation that then and until the mid-1960s we used in church activities, it said "charity" instead of "love."

The pastor always recommended that we do the translation ourselves and read love instead of charity. That, and many other of his teachings, allow me to understand today that we had a pastor ahead of his time.

Living According to the Circumstances

There was no activity of the church and its departments that did not have the presence, help, and necessary guidance of our pastor. He felt part of every action, and not to interfere, modify, or criticize it, but to express his solidarity, understanding, and affection.

A marked calling of Grego was his missionary work. He worked from Camagüey at various times, providing help to the congregations of Guáimaro, Martí, and Florida, and Friday after Friday, he traveled to Vertientes until that mission became a church. Tuesdays and Thursdays at night, you could find him preaching in the neighborhood missions, especially in Garrido, Nadales, or Cándido González, although in the course of his ministry in Camagüey, he passed through many other places around the city with his patient service and his well-versed preaching.

The economic situation of that family was precarious. The salary that my pastor received from the Board was laughable, but he managed to increase his finances by selling honey from beehives that he had in the small country house of the church janitor, Enrique Corsino. I remember that when he visited us, he often brought a little gallon of honey that my grandmother bought from him.

Gregorich was also a visiting pastor. I think he came to my house month after month. My grandmother called all the members of the family to attend to him, and if by chance there was a visitor, she urged them to stay during the time, never very long, that Grego dedicated to us. I remember that, on those visits, when I was a child, she insisted that I memorize Psalm 1... which I never did.

I do not remember that he played leading roles in the conventional structure, but I do remember that as I was already a delegate to some of the assemblies of the Baptist Convention of Eastern Cuba, he spoke in moments of great tensions and that these dissipated with his intervention, characterized by calling to love, understanding and good relationships amid diversity. He judged that his role was to conciliate the sometimes heated discussions of the Conventional Assemblies.

In the so-called business meetings (church assemblies for internal affairs), he was very fair, listened to all opinions, allowed dissent, and was not partial to any of the sides.

There was one exception, which I do not forget despite the young age I was then. It was debated whether the temple would be built first for the Garrido mission or that of Nadales.

The congregation was divided. Heated arguments broke out, and two people even disrespected each other. Grego said, "Here we have lost the guidance of the Spirit, I do not feel strong enough to continue presiding over this meeting."

Living According to the Circumstances

Suddenly, someone rebuked him, "If you believe that the Spirit is not with us and that you do not have the conditions to preside, then call us to prayer so that the Spirit guides us."

Humbly, he accepted the criticism, invited prayer, and prayed. I seem to remember the meaning of the prayer and the expressions in his voice. The Spirit manifested itself, and the meeting ended appropriately, even though the agreement – to build first in Nadales and later in Garrido – was against what I considered correct.

An important aspect of his ministry was work with congregations of Haitian origin that existed throughout the province. He enjoyed working there, even without really having that responsibility. He sometimes spent several days visiting them. He slept in their homes or shelters, ate the same as them, and walked long days to preach, get married, baptize, give communion. I witnessed occasions in which he returned tired and with broken health. He suffered from diabetes and, in those days, violated the diet. His faithful companion, Consuelo, censured him, criticized him, and admonished him, driven by the love she had for him and the desire to help preserve his broken health.

The response I heard on more than one occasion was, "Consuelo, it is my vocation, God has called me to do it. He will give me the strength I need and the health that is essential for this".

Living According to the Circumstances

Rafael Gregorich was my pastor during the first twenty-five years of my existence. Before, he was the pastor of my parents and my grandmother, América Pérez.

That Servant of God called to the pastorate, only told me three times, "God bless you", but when he did it, that beautiful sentence had a deep, real, and necessary meaning. I remember that the first time was on March 25, 1962. I had just concluded the funeral service for my grandmother America, prepared in advance by her before her departure to her heavenly abode. Grego went out with me to the central patio of our house at Bembeta 585.

With marked emotion, he told me, "How flowered Doña América's garden is today! All her plants have given her the most beautiful tributes." I couldn't hold back the tears. He hugged me tightly and said, "God bless you."

The second time was on September 10, 1965. I went looking for him a little before noon, he was in the temple. I told him, "Grego, I'm leaving for Ciego de Ávila in a while, I'm getting married on Sunday the 12th. I'm very sorry that you're not the one to do it, but you know that Marino Santos is the pastor of Ormara, and I must respect her points of view. But how I would have liked you to accompany us that day!" He hugged me again and said quietly, "God bless you!"

Living According to the Circumstances

The third time was the night of July 3, 1966. Ormara and I had gone to dinner at the La Volanta restaurant. We wanted to enjoy the night before I joined the UMAP. At dawn on the 4th, I would have to report to leave. We were on our way to our apartment on San Esteban Street, and we entered the pastoral house. Grego was getting ready to sleep.

I called him aside and told him the situation we were facing, which, although it was not unknown to him, we wanted to reiterate it to him. He looked at us with his peculiarly deep, expressive, loving gaze, and for the third time, he hugged me and said, "God bless you!"

The Sunday before his departure, he preached, as he did every week. His niece Ester, whom he and Consuelo had practically raised, had told me in one of my UMAP passes, "Uncle is going to die in the pulpit, he can no longer continue preaching and pastoring the church. His death is going to surprise one of these days". And so it was, on Tuesday, he got sick and went to the hospital, God called him into his presence.

His funeral, in the temple of the church that he pastored, was a demonstration of affection not only from the First Baptist Church of Camagüey but from the entire evangelical community and the people in general.

The Catholic bishop, Monsignor Adolfo Rodríguez, entered the central path of the temple with his episcopal habit, arrived where good Consuelo was sitting, hugged her, and whispered a message of trust and hope in her ear. Then he spoke commendably of the "simple and humble worker who has earned the favor of this town."

Contrary to city legislation, the burial was done on foot. A sea of people accompanied Grego to the cemetery, and there, the Reverend Marino Santos Martínez, at the time President of the Baptist Convention of Eastern Cuba, delivered one of his most eloquent messages. "Here we have come to say see you later to the pastor, to the teacher, to the companion, to the worker... exemplary father, loving husband, hardworking pastor...".

From that funeral, I remember his children, with Isis at the piano, singing a hymn of hope and faith. There was no trembling voice. They all knew very well that the biblical expression "good and faithful servant... enter into the joy of your Lord" was becoming a reality.

Gilberto Prieto Socarrás (1936-2014)

When we moved to Ciego de Ávila in September 1968, Reverend Prieto held the pastorate of the First Baptist Church. He was born near that city, in a sugarcane colony belonging to the then Algodones sugar mill, today Orlando González. He was the son of humble parents and a member of a long family from which came out three workers from the vineyard of the Lord, all with a beautiful history in the Baptist Convention of Eastern Cuba.

Gilberto, as we affectionately called him, was married to Sister Nérida Rodés Companioni, who, born in Banes, had known the Lord since her youth, and together they had prepared for the ministry. His first pastorate had been in Banes itself, even without having entered the Baptist Seminary of Eastern Cuba.

Then, once married, and while he was studying, he unexpectedly proceeded to take up the pastorate in Ciego de Ávila.

When his previous pastor, Marino Santos Martínez, left to occupy the rectorship of the Seminary, the church elected the Reverend Dante Sánchez Salazar, at the time pastor in Campechuela, to occupy the pastorate. He was never able to assume it. If he had left the pastoral house at that point in the current province of Granma, it would have ceased to be the property of the Church due to certain bureaucratic obstacles.

Dante preferred to continue there and rejected the invitation from the church of Ciego de Ávila. Then, a young man recently graduated from the Seminary came to cooperate with the congregation, his name was Joel Rosales Cortés, and who immediately gained the favor and recognition of the congregation but flatly refused to accept the invitation to be

Living According to the Circumstances

elected as pastor of the church. It was then that, at the suggestion of the Convention board, the church accepted the young pastor Prieto.

Gilberto and Nérida were accompanied by their three children: Lidia and Noemí, twins – fearless and affectionate girls! – and Gilbertico, restless, expressive, and affectionate like his sisters and, of course, like his parents.

Gilberto was a pastor in every sense of the word. I never considered him a great preacher, his messages were more of a colloquial way of sharing the truths of the Gospel. He was a missionary by vocation and an evangelist by love for those who did not know the Lord, but perhaps the main characteristic of this unforgettable Servant of God was his affability and his people skills.

I remember that a few days after he was placed in Ciego de Ávila, we went out together to visit people in the church who were new to the Gospel.

On the corner of Maceo and Libertad, I greeted a friend from Camagüey who was passing through the city. Gilberto greeted him with the same effusiveness as me.

We continued on our way, but surprised by his greeting, I asked him, "Did you know that boy?"

To which he replied, "No, it's the first time I've seen him, but there's no reason why I wouldn't greet him as if I'd known him forever."

In Prieto I had a companion, a friend, as well as a good pastor. Sometimes he would visit me before one of the members' meetings in which some complicated issue was going to be discussed in which I would undoubtedly take a position, not always coinciding with the majority.

He visited me to tell me what was on his agenda and, on occasions, to tell me, "Don't talk about this matter, leave it to me."

The church flourished under his pastorate, precisely at the time when misunderstanding and political segregation damaged the evangelizing effort of the Church in Cuba. He was patient in the face of confrontations that he had to face, and even when they were unfair, he had no words of offense or condemnation.

Of course, he was energetic and defended the position of the Church with dignity and decorum. His wife was the ideal helper who made possible many of the achievements of Gilberto's pastorate.

I believe I have learned from him much of what I later used in my more than twenty years of active pastorate, and even when the interpretation of God, our theologies were not coincident, we knew how to understand each other, never separating ourselves due to that disparity. In short, we learned to live together in the midst of diversity.

There was no task in the church from which he and his wife were absent. All work areas were shared by both, no matter the effort they required, the hours they demanded, or the efforts that were needed. If they were caught late at night, they would lay Gilbertico on a bench and then carry him while the twins, who never slept during one of those long nights, did their thing, to the mortification of some and the joy of others, among whom I found myself.

Gilberto was like a son to Doña Estefanía Machado, Ormara's grandmother. She called him many times privately to exhort, advise, or congratulate him.

As soon as she asked to speak to him alone, Gilberto immediately went to meet her, from whom he always told me that he was blessed. When he was no longer our pastor, I realized more intensely the extent of his simplicity and his humility.

In 1971, the church in Manzanillo called him to the pastorate. When they told him, he asked me to keep it a secret and told me, "I think it is the right time to leave Ciego de Ávila. A pastor should not change churches when there are problems when work is slow when something is wrong. We are in a very beautiful moment in the life of this church, this is how I believe I must accept the call of Manzanillo".

Although what he said was pure truth, and his arguments were very solid, I refuted them. I didn't agree with him leaving us, and it wasn't just my opinion. Gilberto was very loved by the entire congregation.

His farewell was a general mourning. All the neighbors cried, they said goodbye to him with tears and phrases of gratitude, and the church accepted his decision out of discipline and also to respect his points of view.

Melvin Puebla Rodríguez (b1942)

Melvin was born in the Gospel in his native Manzanillo. At the end of his adolescence, when the Reverend Juan Entenza pastored that congregation, his son, Samuel – who was also a pastor later – and Melvin established a deep relationship of affection and companionship.

Melvin worked as a messenger for a cable company, which gave him time to investigate faith. He acquired extensive knowledge and delved into the study of the Bible with his pastor. He entered the Baptist Seminary of Eastern Cuba, and from the beginning there, he distinguished himself from the rest of the students. He was an insatiable researcher, a seeker of broad cultural horizons, and a constant reader of great works of universal literature. Over time, he stood out as someone with a theological thought that did not coincide with that of the majority of his fellow students.

During his student years, he participated in meetings with Christians of other denominations, including Roman Catholics, and that ecumenical breadth continued to open the horizons of his theological interpretation.

He was called to the ranks of the UMAP and there he continued in search of an interpretation of God more in line with his contemporaneity.

In the end, he concluded his studies at the Seminary and was sent to pastor several congregations in the Sagua de Tánamo hills.

The church of Ciego de Ávila called him to the ministry in 1971 after having exhausted the list it had prepared of candidates for the pastorate: Elmer Lavastida, Joel Rosales, Rafael Gregorich Sánchez. Melvin, who was the last on the list, accepted, the church chose him and waited for him for four months of uncertainty. He arrived without prior notice, participated in Sunday School, and the church secretary, Floripe Martín, who did not know him, welcomed "the young man who visits us."

He held the pastorate with his wife, Elba Terrero, also a graduate of the Eastern Baptist Seminary, who had known the

Lord since she was a child through the teachings of her family, residing in Baracoa.

A few months after the Melvin's installation as pastor of the First Church in Ciego de Ávila, his theological interpretation, his liturgical script, and his praxis of faith changed radically.

One day he visited our house and brought me as a gift a *Dictionary of Religion* from the Economic Culture Fund of Mexico that I consulted very frequently, and to Ormara some records with music by Johann Sebastián Bach. He surprised us with the gift of things that we knew were very dear to him.

To our questions, he replied, "I don't need these things, I've gotten rid of my books and my records, I just need a Bible and a Bible dictionary."

I cannot say that Melvin's pastorate contributed to my formation. On the contrary, it was a time of confrontations and disagreements. Melvin adopted a position of isolation, he did not participate in the activities programmed by the different areas of the church, and he even refused to take part in the Sunday School, which Ormara directed, neither as a teacher nor even to make announcements or give guidance in the closing.

The church was divided and therefore, the testimony of unity required "for the world to believe" was significantly affected. We broke the relationships of companionship and friendship. I tried not to be forced to greet him at the end of the service, and although I did not do it publicly, in my family, I censured his ministry.

I was separated from the church in early 1978 when I was a student at *Codrington College* in Barbados. Upon my return, the situation became unsustainable and the distancing forced me, along with a large group of people gradually separated from the Church, to stop participating in its life.

There were many years of uncommunication, but on January 1, 1992, I told Ormara, "This year can't end without reconciling with Melvin".

It was on November 22 that I called him on the phone, "Melvin, this is Noel, I need to talk with you." To which he replied, "Do it tomorrow, you can come to church."

Without thinking, I responded positively. He told me, "Come down to Máximo Gómez Street at ten in the morning, the door will be open, and I will be waiting for you." I attended the appointment on time, we talked, I apologized for my inappropriate attitude, and told him that I was to blame for what happened. He, for his part, admitted that the fault was of both of us. I told him to seal the moment with a prayer.

At the end, he extended his hand to me, "No, Melvin, the hand is not enough, let's give each other a hug." So it was.

Eduardo González Hernández (b1971)

Living According to the Circumstances

For a retiring pastor, staying in the church of which he was pastor is complicated and not always feasible. There are many cases of frustration and sadness among those of us who have had to leave the pastorate in the hands of another person who is not always a continuator of what has been done and who sometimes feels dwarfed by the figure he took over.

That has not been my case. Upon my retirement, the church elected by 93 percent of the votes Eduardito, the son of Sister Nora Hernández, who was a member of the First Baptist Church in Ciego de Ávila and a friend of Ormara since youth.

Together with her, we worked in that church until she left it in the 1970s for various reasons. We saw her two children grow up. Eduardito, the oldest, intrepid, jovial, and friendly, joined the Emmanuel church when we began the activities at the Libertad Street location.

From the beginning he showed his gifts, including his people skills, learned from his mother. Little by little, he took an active part in church activities. He never objected to any task, but, on the contrary, he assumed it even before it was assigned to him.

In 2006, the Canaán Baptist Church, in the municipality of Bolivia, found itself without a pastor, because who was in charge of that task was separated from his duties by the congregation itself after giving a poor testimony of his faith. I prepared to resume the pastorate of that congregation, of which I had been the founder and first pastor, and to do so, I made it a condition that Eduardito be my assistant. He had a transport that could be used easily, and, on most occasions, I thought he would take on the task.

To my surprise, the church did not accept my proposal and instead decided to choose Eduardito as pastor and me as his "mentor."

The idea, I say with joy, had my complete approval. This is how this young man began in the arts of spiritually guiding a group of brothers and sisters. Later he began to study Theology at the Perkins School of Theology in Dallas, Texas, studies that he completed in English, a language that he knows perfectly.

The wide range of my responsibilities in ensuring that disability was part of the agendas of the Churches in Cuba and Latin America required more of my time.

Leaving the active pastorate, even though it was not my desire, became a necessity. On the other hand, I am in favor of the pastorate being in the hands of young people. Those of us who are past retirement age cling to customs, methods, and attitudes that distance new generations from the congregations.

The decision was made, and following the usual process among Baptists, Eduardito was elected, installed, and ordained to the Holy Ministry in May 2009.

Since that date, the one who was the "sheep of my flock" is now my shepherd. His treatment of me has been that of the son we did not have.

Of course, there are moments to applaud and occasions to censure, and the latter "without your right knowing what your left is doing (or saying)" has given us magnificent results.

I edify myself every Sunday with his sermon, which, with rare exceptions, I classify as brilliant and always very contextual. His dynamism and his work method, very different from mine, have brought renewed air to the church of which I am now a part without interfering in any of its administrative and organizational aspects.

The Reverend Eduardo González is still very new to these events, but if his career continues as before, the future of the church he now pastors and those he will pastor in the future is guaranteed.

Living According to the Circumstances

Afterword To The English Edition

Thank you for reading Noel's memoir. You may think that it ended abruptly, and perhaps it did. Of course, his introduction to the book is a good summary and would also make a good ending. So, please reread it if you feel it necessary.

We don't know why Noel ended his book as he did. Perhaps he said all he wanted to say! But here is a possible reason. Being the founding pastor of Emmanuel and shepherding it through its first years was the culmination of Noel's long, complicated, and accomplished life. His last words in the book were about Eduardo González Hernández, who followed Noel as pastor at Emmanuel.

Eduardo is more than a generation younger than Noel. It is obvious that Noel believes Emmanuel is in good hands with Eduardo as its pastor. And knowing Eduardo as we do, we think so as well. So, perhaps in ending the book the way he did, Noel is implying that for him, it was time to "pass the torch" to a new generation of leaders and trust in their leadership. That's a lesson we could all learn. Another thought. We all have more chapters to live in our own lives. Perhaps we can all begin to write those chapters as we live in and into our own circumstances.

We are so happy that we have played a part in bringing Noel's amazing and important memoir to an English-reading audience.

As Noel mentions, we first met him and Ormara in June of 1994, thirty years ago now, when four of us from Northminster Church in Monroe, Louisiana, journeyed to Cuba in search of a church affiliated with the Fraternity of Baptist Churches of Cuba (FIBAC) with which to partner. The progressive Alliance of Baptists in the United States, with which Northminster is affiliated, was encouraging its member churches in this endeavor.

As Noel also mentions, the intention was for us to travel from Havana to the extreme eastern end of the island before coming to a decision. However, when we arrived in Ciego de Avila, met Noel and Ormara and a few other members of the not-yet-officially-constituted Emmanuel Baptist Church, we "fell in love." The rest, as is said, is history. And what a beautiful history.

Over these thirty years, we have visited Emmanuel almost yearly and sometimes twice a year. So, we figure at least thirty times. On multiple occasions Noel and Ormara have visited Northminster and stayed with us in our homes in Monroe. We have been to at least three annual gatherings of the Alliance of Baptists together, twice in Washington, DC, and once in Raleigh, NC.

Living According to the Circumstances

Over the years, we have communicated frequently, first by mail, then by email, by at least monthly telephone calls and now by WhatsApp as well. We have lots of stories!

One story is from very early in our partnership. After our visit to Ciego de Avila, we were traveling back to Havana, about a six-hour drive, in Ormara's Soviet-built Lada. Our new friend José Máure, a member at Emmanuel, was our driver, and Noel, the "navigator." Máure had never driven to nor in Havana.

At one point along the highway, Noel said, "Máure, there is a large pothole about one kilometer ahead. Please be on the lookout." Sure enough, about a kilometer ahead, there was a huge pothole, large enough to swallow a small car, and fortunately, we avoided it. As we neared Havana, Noel gave directions to our destination and, along the way, pointed out places of interest! How?

Over the years Noel and Ormara have become our dear friends and like family to us. We have said on many occasions that Noel can "see" better than most persons who are sighted. And by that, we don't mean by just being able to navigate his way to Havana and all the other multiple places he has been in the world. We mean, as Rev. Stanard said so eloquently in his Forward, that Noel is imbued with "vision." That vision has guided, challenged and encouraged Noel in all the circumstances of the life he has lived. It is indeed the "vision" that comes from and through his living the faith *of* Christ to help bring about God's reign on this good earth.

Another story is Craig's story, and so I (Craig) will tell this story in the first person. In 1996, Noel and Ormara were staying with me in my home on their first visit with us and Northminster. Noel asked me if I had a typewriter. He wanted to write some letters while they were there. As it turned out, I did have an Underwood Standard typewriter my parents had given me in high school that had been sitting unused in various closets for twenty-three years since I graduated from law school. It had served me well over the years including my having typed all my law school exams and the bar exams on it with success. But, at the law firm, I had access to an electric typewriter, and thus, the old Underwood Standard had sat unused for all those years. I got it out of the closet, bought a new ribbon for it, and set Noel up at my kitchen table. I thought I was a fast typist, but I couldn't hold a candle to him. He typed a lot of letters in those few days at my house. And then, I put the Underwood Standard back in the closet.

Before our next visit to Ciego de Avila, which I believe was later that year, we were visiting with Noel and Ormara by phone. We asked if there was anything they needed that we could bring with us. With some slight hesitation and a touch of sheepishness, Noel said, "I would love it if you would bring me that typewriter." So, I packed the Underwood Standard, all twenty-five pounds of it, in my luggage and safely delivered it to Noel in Cuba.

For several years, he was very busy with writing letters, papers, and such in his various roles as pastor at Emmanuel and with the Cuban Council of Churches and the World Council of Churches. And then, of course, the computer arrived and, for Noel, an even more useful "talking" computer. But fortunately, the Underwood Standard found a new life at Canaan Baptist Church in Bolivia where it continued to serve faithfully for many years.

Our point: Despite his loss of sight, the written word has come to be an important tool of expression for this brilliant, gifted, and caring human being. This is clearly obvious in this particular work of his. And it is definitely obvious in the many, many sermons, Bible studies, lessons, papers dealing with disability and other subjects and letters he has written over the years. His early beautiful letters to us and later his carefully crafted emails, always newsy, of which there have been many over the years and to which we always look forward, are eloquent expressions of his devotion to friends and to ministry. The written word is a marvelous thing!

Thank you again, Noel, for sharing your life with the world through the pages of your memoir. May we all, like you, live, grow, be challenged, and ACT according to our own circumstances. Thanks be to God!

Living According to the Circumstances

Craig Henry

D. H. Clark

Monroe, Louisiana U.S.A

August 6, 2024

About The Author

Noel Fernández Collot, born in Camagüey, Cuba, on February 28, 1942, son and grandson of the members of the First Baptist Church of that city. From adolescence, he was a leader in the work of that congregation.

Later, together with his wife Ormara Nolla Cao, also a member of a family of the same denomination, they were the promoters, for several years, of the work with the adolescents of the Eastern Baptist Convention of Cuba.

In the early 1960s, following the Cuban Revolution, he was ordered to the Military Units to Aid Production, UMAP, a kind of work camp where religious leaders from different institutions attended along with gay men, pimps, and people of dubious morals. Despite the difficulty, Noel considered it a blessing because it allowed him to know the life of this universe of people.

In 1990, he was the founding pastor of the EMMANUEL Baptist Church in the city of Ciego de Ávila, work that allowed him to plant six churches in the province of Ciego de Avila and missionary work in 12 other places.

Noel has been blind since age 30 from retinitis pigmentosa. In 1990, he proposed to the Council of Churches of Cuba the creation of a space for pastoral care for people with disabilities, and the request to coordinate that program was approved.

Since the early 1980s, he has been linked to the work of the World Council of Churches (WCC) in the field of disability. Since 1989, he was a member of the ECUMENICAL NETWORK IN DEFENSE OF PEOPLE WITH DISABILITIES of that organization. He was a member of its Coordination Group responsible for coordinating that network in Latin America, work carried out until 2015.

He has developed workshops, seminars, and short courses on the topic of disability in various theological institutions in Latin America.

+ +

The photograph above was taken of Noel and Ormara in 2022 outside their first apartment in Camagüey.